THE SPIRIT OF THOREAU

———

Uncommon Learning

The Spirit of Thoreau

SPONSORED BY THE THOREAU SOCIETY

Wesley T. Mott, Series Editor

❧

Uncommon Learning:
Thoreau on Education

Material Faith:
Thoreau on Science

Elevating Ourselves:
Thoreau on Mountains

Uncommon Learning

THOREAU ON EDUCATION

Edited by Martin Bickman

Foreword by Jonathan Kozol

A Mariner Original

Houghton Mifflin Company

BOSTON NEW YORK

1999

Library of Congress Cataloging-in-Publication Data

Thoreau, Henry David, 1817–1862.
Uncommon learning : Thoreau on education / edited by
Martin Bickman ; foreword by Jonathan Kozol.
p. cm — (The spirit of Thoreau)
ISBN 0-395-94797-9
1. Thoreau, Henry David, 1817–1862 — Quotations.
2. Education — Quotations, maxims, etc.
I. Bickman, Martin, 1945- .   II. Title.   III. Series: Thoreau,
Henry David, 1817–1862. Spirit of Thoreau.
PS3042.B35 1999   99-12985
818'.309—dc21   CIP

Book design by Anne Chalmers
Type: Bulmer (Monotype)

Printed in the United States of America
QBP 10 9 8 7 6 5 4 3 2 1

Jonathan Kozol

It is the destiny of many of our greatest writers and most interesting thinkers to be read selectively and used exploitatively in later years by those who aren't content to celebrate their glories but instead attempt to package them in ways that will accommodate contemporary fashions or sectarian beliefs.

In the case of Thoreau's views on education, this is a particularly dangerous temptation. His ideas on childhood and education and his actual experience as a schoolteacher offer a diverse display of marvelously bold, inventive, and sometimes deliciously iconoclastic practices and points of view, as well as some that are remarkably old-fashioned and traditional. Almost all have been appropriated by a wide diversity of pedagogic partisans over the years to reinforce and, frequently, romanticize their own most cherished ideologies.

Thoreau's emphasis, for instance, upon lived experience as an essential element of education—one that is more fruitful, often, than the benefits to be derived from formal methods of instruction—has been used repeatedly to justify entirely random and unstructured educational approaches in which discipline and rigor are eschewed, "book learning" scorned, and the role of educator whittled down to the diminished point where teachers are reluctant to assign a book, insist on its completion, or demand some evidence that children have in fact learned something from its reading.

It is salutary, therefore, to remind ourselves that Thoreau's pedagogic views, as dedicated as he was to freedom and to individual and practical experience for children and adults alike, did not exclude some rigorous instructional approaches that contemporary libertarians have tended to dismiss and even ridicule. It is also easily forgotten that Thoreau himself, who rewrote *Walden* seven times before he had it in a form that satisfied his sense of artistry, worked with a steadfast discipline and purposeful intentionality on almost everything he did. This willingness to labor hard and long, and to insist on the same kind of diligence from pupils, is not always recognized by those who, in our own day, sometimes claim to wear his mantle. The notion that a child often learns "by doing" is confused too frequently with the calamitous idea that children *never* learn by reading or by listening or writing and rewriting in the same painstaking way that Thoreau did.

Thoreau, admittedly, would now and then refer to formal regimens of education with a lot of likable irreverence; but in the work he did with children he used common sense and held them to the same exacting standards that good teachers try to uphold in the classroom even now. Walter Harding notes, for instance, that when Thoreau and his brother ran a school in Concord, pupils would be questioned as to what they wished to learn.

When a student answered that he wished to study Latin, Greek, and mathematics, he would then be told he'd be successful only if he would "obey our rules" and "do what we require." The school's curriculum was rigorous, according to the students. "In the morning," one boy wrote his father, "I recite Solid Geometry. . . . Geography comes next. . . . Grammar comes next." In the afternoon, he said, "Mr. Henry's classes" studied algebra and Latin. In Latin, he reported, they were studying the life of Alcibiades, irregular verbs, and "conjugation in the grammar." Small errors in their Latin grammar drew stiff reprimands from Mr. Henry, as a student recollected later.

What now are known as "field trips" to the country-side surrounding Concord were a part of the curriculum as well. Children studied plants and animals firsthand and not exclusively through the use of texts. Thoreau delighted in this aspect of his teaching, and some of his most invigorating writing draws upon the hours that he spent outside the classroom with his pupils. But he also was a hard taskmaster in traditional respects and tended to be "rigid . . . in exacting good work," as one of his students noted later. The overall curriculum that he enforced was not at all rhapsodic or unstructured but a great deal like the course of study found today in classrooms of the most respected public schools, some of which — historic Boston Latin School, for instance — he would find exceedingly familiar.

Thoreau is paradoxically appropriated nowadays by very bitter critics of the public schools, many of whom are ideologically conservative, who note — correctly — that some of his criticisms of the role of government in education are consistent with their own. But for all his independent spirit and his jubilant defiance of collective obligations, he espoused the morally commanding view that social orders must provide an education of all children and must do so in collective ways, by which he also made very clear that he meant public education. For all the rich and lovely inconsistencies within his published work and journals, his belief in public education comes through with a glowing and persistent eloquence.

In the long run, it is healthy to remind ourselves that Thoreau's most abiding legacy to educators, whether at the grade-school level or that of the university, lies not in an isolated phrase or passage on specific practices of teaching. It is the spirit of the man, the freshness and the merriment, the sheer delight he takes in mischievous self-contradiction, the defiant humor, and the ultimately irreducible morality of his existence that remain the gift of joy and courage he has left to us.

The greatest damage we could do to this perpetually energizing gift is to imprison it in any deadening container of sectarian opinion. His words would stubbornly denounce us if we sought to use them in this way. "I desire to speak somewhere *without* bounds," he insisted in some of the final words of *Walden*; he managed to succeed in this as only a few writers of his era did and as too few have managed to do since. It is his boundlessness that has survived the dustiness of decades. If we leave him free to wander without boundaries, it seems safe to say that he'll continue to delight, infuriate, inform, and educate his fellow citizens and fellow human beings for centuries to come. To let him stand for what he was—"a face of bronze," as he once put it, held to expectations — is perhaps the only way to honor his tenacious independence and to prove ourselves his students in a way that will not utterly dishonor the best lesson he has left us.

JONATHAN KOZOL, author of a number of prizewinning books on childhood and education, continues to read Thoreau with teenage students.

Thoreau and the Tradition of the Active Mind

MARTIN BICKMAN

Thoreau's relation to education as an institution has been problematic. He entered the teaching profession early, as an undergraduate, and left it a few years later, when he closed the private school he had conducted with his brother. Although, as we shall see, there were external reasons for this action, Thoreau's departure from teaching also resulted from disillusion with the conventional classroom, a growing sense that it prevented learning rather than fostering it. Also, placing the focus where it really should be, he increasingly came to feel that "it is strange that men are in such haste to get fame as teachers rather than knowledge as learners" (10 March 1856, *Journal*). He spent the rest of his life learning and writing — the two were usually the same for him — but he never lost his concern for teaching, both envisioning better ways to go about it and launching a powerful critique of the way it was usually done: "What does education often do! — It makes a straight-cut ditch of a free, meandering brook" (after 31 October 1850, *Journal*).

Because he stands outside the mainstream of educational practice, Thoreau can help us transcend the false oppositions that have arisen between traditionalists and progressives, between the advocates of "basics" and those of openness and creativity—between the curriculum and the child, as Dewey put it. For Thoreau envisioned and enacted a necessary synthesis, a working dialectic of thinking and doing, of transmitting old cultural forms and creating new ones, and of democratic schooling and the pursuit of excellence.

Thoreau can help us reconcile these self-defeating oppositions because he himself was both a doer and a thinker, an innovative teacher and a speculative writer. Although his career as a classroom teacher ended early, he continued to reflect on the process of education throughout the voluminous writings that recorded and shaped his own low-key but intensely experienced life. He embodied—some even say invented—the notion of continuing education or lifelong learning. He was a pioneer in adult education through his work as both an organizer and a lecturer in the lyceum movement and through the intellectual activism fostered by the transcendentalist movement. The plea, included here, in the "Reading" chapter of *Walden* for "uncommon schools," in which the citizens of a village pool their resources for common scholarly advancement, is one of the earliest and most eloquent calls for state support of cultural activities. But Thoreau was an advocate for *continuing* education more fundamentally in the sense that he knew that no formulation or system is sufficient or permanent, that to be responsively alive is to be a perpetual learner, always aware of both the possibilities and the limits of one's current knowledge. Thoreau remained not only a learner but also a learner of how he learned, keeping in his journal a series of what we would now call metacognitive reflections. The journal is one of the most thorough and detailed records we have of what Emerson called "life passed through the fire of thought" (*Essays,* 85), of productive alternations between world and mind, experiencing and conceptualizing, living and writing.

The fact that Thoreau's educational philosophy was rooted in his own immediate experience does not mean that this philosophy was crankily eccentric or narrowly personal. Indeed, one of the main tasks of this introduction is to show that Thoreau's vision of education can best be explained and appreciated by viewing it as part of a larger movement in American intellectual life, what I call the "tradition of the active mind." The term "tradition," though, is somewhat paradoxical here, since this confluence of thinking seeks to free itself from the grip of the past in favor of the immediate act of the mind encountering the world; the active mind trusts its own workings over any previous formulations, whether by itself or others.

But, however vexed the relationship between the notion of the active mind and historical indebtedness, it does have a discernible genealogy. It has played a vital part in our educational history, although ignored or suppressed by forces Thoreau constantly battled: unthinking routine, institutional inertia, and blind authoritarianism. This antitraditional tradition can be traced from Thoreau's own mentors, Ralph Waldo Emerson and Bronson Alcott, through William James and John Dewey, to a number of more recent educators. It views the site of schooling as a place where the tensions that beleaguer our existence — body and soul, self and society, emotion and intellect — can be reconciled. The actual embodiments of this view, such as Alcott's Temple School, Thoreau's Concord Academy, Dewey's Laboratory School, and Dennison's First Street School, have been on a small scale and short-lived. Yet these experiments have kept alive the possibility of schools as genuine democratic and intellectual communities, living realizations of what Allen Ginsberg has called "the lost America of love." This introduction will show how Thoreau's work and this larger but repressed tradition can mutually explain and clarify each other. It will sketch out first his own teaching career and then relate that career and his later writings to this lineage of the active mind.

Thoreau began teaching before his own formal education was complete. As a sophomore at Harvard College, he took advantage of a recent faculty ruling that allowed students a leave of absence to teach school for up to thirteen weeks. It is likely that Thoreau took this opportunity primarily for financial reasons, but he probably also wanted a break from an educational system he often found diffuse, rigid, and superficial. He later said that Harvard taught all the branches of learning but none of the roots (Albee, *Remembrances of Emerson,* 31), and he noted in *Walden* that he had been enrolled in a course in navigation that was so removed from the concrete realities that he wasn't even aware of having taken it. So in the fall of 1835 Thoreau applied to teach in Canton, a town south of Boston, where he was interviewed by the young minister, Orestes Brownson, who was on the verge of fame as a fiery transcendentalist with his *New Views of Christianity and the Church,* to be published the next year. Little is known of this first teaching episode, except that whatever Thoreau's experience with his seventy students he was not discouraged from teaching as a future career. And whatever he learned about education, his development was probably fostered more by his study of German and his conversations with Brownson, the very model of an intellectual activist who, like Karl Marx, wanted to change the world, not just understand it.

After graduating from Harvard College in the summer of 1837, Thoreau, now twenty, began his shortest and most notorious teaching stint. In that year of financial panic he was fortunate enough to land a position in his native Concord as the teacher at the Center School, the main public college preparatory school. This post was traditionally offered to a recent Harvard graduate, but Thoreau, unlike many of his predecessors, was not just biding his time en route to becoming a lawyer or minister. Dick O'Connor, who has most thoroughly studied Thoreau's brief tenure here, writes that he "had some ideas of his own about teaching that he was eager to put into practice. He fully intended to stay in teaching for several years, perhaps — after a year of public school experience and self-directed study — taking a position in a private academy" ("Thoreau in the Town School," 153–54). But during his first few days, Thoreau was visited by Nehemiah Ball, one of the three members of the school committee. Ball found the activity and noise level of the classroom too high and instructed the young teacher to use corporal punishment more often. Stung by the criticism, Thoreau applied the ferule (a stick for rapping on the hand rather than a cowhide strip for flogging, which the school did not have) to six students, some chosen at random, some punished for minor infractions. That evening he turned in his resignation.

Like much of Thoreau's experience, this act of uncivil obedience was not as memorable or original in itself

(Bronson Alcott had preceded him both in criticizing corporal punishment and in not paying his poll tax) as his later verbal formulation of it; in seeking a new teaching job, he wrote to Brownson: "I have even been disposed to regard the cowhide as a nonconductor. Methinks that, unlike the electric wire, not a single spark of truth is ever transmitted through its agency to the slumbering intellect it would address" (30 December 1837, *Correspondence*). But more significant than this negative critique is his positive vision of schooling in the same letter:

> I would make education a pleasant thing both to the teacher and the scholar. This discipline, which we allow to be the end of life, should not be one thing in the schoolroom, and another in the street. We should seek to be fellow students with the pupil, and should learn of, as well as with him, if we would be most helpful to him. But I am not blind to the difficulties of the case; it supposes a degree of freedom which rarely exists. It hath not entered into the heart of man to conceive the full import of that word — Freedom — not a paltry Republican freedom, with a *posse comitatus* at his heels to administer it in doses as to a sick child — but a freedom proportionate to the dignity of his nature — a freedom that shall make him feel that he is a man among men, and responsible only to that Reason of which he is a particle, for his thoughts and his actions.

Instead of any disillusionment with teaching, Thoreau articulates an inspiriting vision that he was to apply to the rest of his educational work. This vision is a remarkable epitome of the values inherent in the tradition of the active mind, having particular affinities with the thought of John Dewey. Like Dewey, Thoreau chooses to see education not simply as a means, a preparation for something else, but as intrinsically valuable. Both men assert a fundamental continuity between the schoolroom and the street, between the process of learning and the rest of experience. And both seek to go beyond the conventional dichotomy of teacher and student, suggesting that the teacher can learn with and from the student. In other words, education should not simply transmit an existing culture but creatively reconstruct it. Most centrally, both Thoreau and Dewey see education as crucial to democracy and vice versa; for democracy to be a living philosophy, it cannot be expressed only on election day but must be part of every act of building a true community.

Soon after writing this remarkable letter, Thoreau found an opportunity to embody these ideas in practice. After almost a year of unsuccessfully pursuing leads for other teaching positions, he decided, in June 1838, to open his own school. It began modestly in the family home with only four students. When Concord Academy, the private college preparatory school he had attended himself, looked as if it would fold, he was able to rent the building and take over the name. By the next winter the school had enrolled enough students that Henry was able to bring in as a second teacher his older brother, John, who had been teaching on his own in Roxbury.

Although the brothers retained most features of conventional schooling, they supplemented these with a number of activities that moved education beyond the walls of the classrooms. There were frequent field trips, and not just to fields for nature study. The students were taken to the offices of a local paper to watch typesetting and to a gunsmith to watch the regulating of gunsights. In the spring, each student had a small plot of plowed land to plant. In the fall of 1840 Henry brought in surveying instruments to teach his students yet another kind of field work in organizing a survey of Fairhaven Hill. Surveying, as Thomas Pynchon was later to illustrate in *Mason & Dixon,* is a wonderful synecdoche for the imposition of human order on the natural world, a way to explore the relation between mathematical concept and physical reality.

But rather than just listing activities, we can get a better sense of Thoreau's teaching by following him through an entire sequence. This account of a river trip was reported by F. B. Sanborn, one of Thoreau's early biographers, who himself later ran a progressive school in Concord:

> Henry Thoreau called attention to a spot on the rivershore, where he fancied the Indians had made their fires, and perhaps had a fishing village. . . . "Do you see," said Henry, "anything here that would be likely to attract Indians to this spot?" One boy said, "Why, here is the river for their fishing"; another pointed to the woodland near by, which could give them game. "Well, is there anything else?" pointing out a small rivulet that must come, he said, from a spring not far off, which could furnish water cooler than the river in summer; and a hillside above it that would keep off the north and northwest wind in winter. Then, moving inland a little farther, and looking carefully about, he struck his spade several times, without result.

Presently, when the boys began to think their young teacher and guide was mistaken, his spade struck a stone. Moving forward a foot or two, he set his spade in again, struck another stone, and began to dig in a circle. He soon uncovered the red, fire-marked stones of the long-disused Indian fireplace; thus proving that he had been right in his conjecture. Having settled the point, he carefully covered up his find and replaced the turf,—not wishing to have the domestic altar of the aborigines profaned by mere curiosity. (*The Life of Henry David Thoreau,* 205–6)

Here Thoreau helps his students read the natural landscape as carefully and closely as a page of Cicero. They are asked to not merely appreciate its beauty but to make logical inferences about its possible relations to the human world, to formulate hypotheses and test those hypotheses through further activity. His own actions model an intellectual curiosity about the immediate world we move through, a willingness to take the risk of being proven wrong, and a respect for the past and other cultures. He enacts and embodies these qualities, modeling instead of preaching them.

On 1 April 1841, the brothers closed their school because of John's failing health from tuberculosis, the disease from which Henry was eventually to die also. Later, Henry tutored Emerson's nephew on Staten Island for a few homesick months in 1843. And informally he was a wonderful teacher to many of the children around him, as documented in detail by two of them, Edward Emerson in *Henry Thoreau as Remembered by a Young Friend* and Louise May Alcott in *Little Men,* where he is fictionalized as Mr. Hyde. But he was never to be a classroom teacher again. On the positive side, he wanted to devote all his energies to his writing. But on the negative side, he had a deep, underlying suspicion of the whole activity of formal education. In his journal he writes: "How vain it is to teach youth, or anybody, truths! They can only learn them after their own fashion, and when they get ready" (31 December 1859, *Journal*).

Thoreau's subsequent involvement with education, then, was primarily as a writer. He did not write a separate single work on the subject, but, as appropriate to one who saw education as continuous with all experience, his insights are found throughout his work, most richly in *Walden* and the journal. In collecting these thoughts on education in one place, this volume reveals the actual power and convergence of Thoreau's educational vision. While some of these passages do indeed contradict others—and it has often been noted that self-contradiction is part of the transcendentalist stance toward immediate honesty and complexity—we can see both the negative comments about existing schools and the envisioning of a positive education as two sides of the same viewpoint, one that comes into sharper focus against the matrix of thought already referred to as the tradition of the active mind.

The first figure chronologically in this tradition is Bronson Alcott, father of Louisa May and the three other little women. In 1834 he opened in Boston, with Elizabeth Peabody, the Temple School, which embodied and anticipated what many educators now believe about the best ways to teach. Instead of rote memorization and recitation from textbooks, the children were asked to shape and share their own thoughts in both journals and class discussions. The education was what we would now call "holistic," since skills like spelling, grammar, and vocabulary were integrated into larger lessons on ethical and spiritual matters.

Alcott's conduct of the classroom and the discussions was sometimes unconsciously manipulative, but he was also much of the time a good listener and a provocative questioner. Although he was not as good a writer as a teacher—his writings tend to be vaporously abstract, ironically violating his own best teaching practices—we are fortunate in having descriptions and transcripts of the school preserved by Elizabeth Peabody in *Record of a School* (1835) and in *Conversations with Children on the Gospels* (1836–37), which appeared under Alcott's name. One sequence in particular shows the strength of his methods:

> Mr. Alcott then recurred to the blackboard and said he would read the scale. This diagram had been altered many times during the quarter. It was intended to systematize the conversations in a degree; and never was presented to the children as a complete map of the mind. Some have objected to these diagrams, as if they would be fetters on the minds of the children. But their constant renewal and changes preclude the possibility of their being regarded as any thing but what they are. After having read the scale through, he began at the end asking the meaning of each word, and as they were defined, he obliterated them, until all were gone. (*Record of a School,* 167)

The scale or diagram, then, is offered not as a self-contained external truth but as a tool to help the students probe, order, and articulate their own experiences. The scheme is offered as hypothetical, provisional, subject to revision. In a final flourish, Alcott even erases each term after it is revisited to emphasize that it is not the verbal construct itself that should be abstracted from the lesson but the entire process, the crucial interplay between experience and concept.

Thoreau owned a copy of *Record of a School* while he was teaching in his own school, and he thought enough of it to send a copy to Isaiah Williams. During this time he came to know Alcott personally, after the Temple School closed in a flurry of controversy and Alcott moved his family to Concord. Louisa May and her older sister were enrolled in the Thoreau brothers' academy, and Henry and Bronson began a long friendship. This educational interaction came full circle when Alcott, who became Concord's school superintendent in 1859, planned to have Thoreau create a textbook based on the local geography and natural history of Concord, to be supplemented by his own guided field trips. In his report for 1861, Alcott writes: "Happily we have a sort of resident Surveyor-General of the town's farms, farmers, animals, and everything else it contains,—who makes more of it than most persons with a continent at their call. Will he just set his ten senses at work upon an illustrated Atlas for the citizens, giving such account of the world they inhabit, with such hints concerning the one he lives in, as he pleases?" (*Essays on Education*, 174). This project was finally thwarted by Thoreau's last illness and death, but it underscored what the two shared: a deep respect for the local and the concrete as the basis of all learning, a hope that education can bring us to our senses, in all senses of this word, and a vision of schooling in which knowledge is as much constructed as transmitted.

If Alcott was more a teacher than a writer or theorist, his qualities were complemented by another of Thoreau's friends, Ralph Waldo Emerson. Emerson's "American Scholar" address, delivered to Thoreau's Harvard College class of 1837, is the earliest major manifesto in the tradition of the active mind. We cannot be sure Thoreau himself was in attendance, but as an undergraduate he had already read Emerson's first book, *Nature* (1836), and upon Thoreau's return to Concord at this time Emerson became a powerful mentor for him. In education, as in other areas, the older man frequently saw Thoreau as embodying and living out his own ideas. Emerson notes in his journal, for example, the boat trip that John and Henry took on one of their vacations from teaching: "Now here are my wise young neighbors who instead of getting like the workmen into a railroad-car where they have not even the activity of holding the reins, have got into a boat which they have built with their own hands, with sails which they have contrived to serve as a tent, & gone up the river Merrimack to live by their wits on the fish of the stream & the berries of the wood. My worthy neighbor Dr. Bartlett expressed a true parental instinct when he desired to send his boy with them to learn something" (*Emerson in His Journals*, 223–24).

"The American Scholar" is sometimes taken primarily as a call for American literary independence, but this theme, already a tired American topos, is trumpeted only at the beginning and the end. More centrally the address is a radical rethinking of the relationship between education and culture. Before philosophical pragmatism and cognitive psychology, Emerson saw learning not as the discovery of preexisting truth but as the process of making knowledge in a constant transaction between the self and the world: "The scholar of the first age received into him the world around; brooded thereon; gave it the arrangement of his own mind, and uttered it again. It came to him life; it went out from him truth" (*Essays,* 56). What is crucial here is the entire process, not just the end product, such as a book or a fixed idea, which can become deadeningly tyrannical if we dwell too long with it rather than immerse ourselves in the cycle: "Each age, it is found, must write its own books. . . . The books of an older period will not fit this. Yet hence arises a grave mischief. The sacredness which attaches to the act of creation,—the act of thought,—is transferred to the record. The poet chanting was felt to be a divine man; henceforward it is settled, the book is perfect; as love of the hero corrupts into worship of his statue" (*Essays,* 56–57).

In this last image, the living hero is frozen into hardness and coldness while the reciprocal emotion of love turns into the one-way abasement of worship. Thoreau was to use more natural, homely metaphors to describe this process of intellectual rigor mortis: "It appears to me that at a very early age—the mind of man—perhaps at the same time with his body, ceases to be elastic. His intellectual power becomes something defined—& limited. He does not think as expansively as he would stretch himself in his growing days—What was flexible sap hardens into heartwood" (2 April 1852, *Journal*). And elsewhere he writes of those who go to Europe to "finish their education," pun intended: "Instead of acquiring nutritious and palatable qualities to their pulp, it is all absorbed into a prematurely hardened shell. They went away squashes, and they return gourds" (30 July 1853, *Journal*).

The worst effect of conventional schooling is to perpetuate and exacerbate this situation. As Emerson writes: "The book, the college, the school of art, the institution of any kind, stop with some past utterance of genius. This is good, say they,—let us hold by this" (*Essays,* 57–58). Thoreau uses a cluster of images for this process, focusing on well-worn paths and ruts. In one journal entry he writes: "Every thought that passes through the mind helps to wear & tear it & to deepen the ruts which as in the streets of Pompeii evince how much it has been used" (7 July 1851, *Journal*). Most poignantly, this figurative rut becomes literal in the path that Thoreau himself wears between his hut and Walden Pond: "I had not lived there a week before my feet wore a path from my door to the pond-side; and though it is five or six years since I trod it, it is still quite distinct. It is true, I fear that others may have fallen into it, and so helped to keep it open. The surface of the earth is soft and impressible by the feet of men; and so with the paths which the mind travels. How worn and dusty, then, must be the highways of the world, how deep the ruts of tradition and conformity!" (*Walden,* 323). Even when the cultural artifact, then, is of one's own making, even when it is as supple and magnificent as a book like *Walden,* we must keep going beyond it. As Emerson writes: "Every thought is also a prison; every heaven is also a prison" (*Essays,* 463).

Emerson and Thoreau, then, as well as the other writers in this tradition, envision an education that does not simply pass on the end results of past cultural creations but that immerses each student in the entire cycle of experiencing, formulating, and then reinstating these formulations back into experience to test, hone, and modify. As Emerson puts it, "Only so much do I know, as I have lived. . . . So much only of life as I know by experience, so much of the wilderness have I vanquished and planted" (*Essays,* 60). And just as crucial as the construction or reconstruction of cultural forms is the continual destruction and transcendence of the confining and limiting old forms, even when—or especially when —they are of our own making. Few writers have been as eloquent as Thoreau about the necessity for this renewal of ignorance in education, as in this sentence, whose very grammatical construction emphasizes not knowing: "I do not know that knowledge amounts to anything more definite than a novel & grand surprise on a sudden revelation of the insufficiency of all that we had called knowledge before." And in *Walden* he writes: "Every man has to learn the points of the compass again as often as he wakes, whether from sleep or any abstraction" (171). Indeed, the entire project of moving out to—and then leaving—Walden Pond, of writing *Walden* but reminding us at the end that "the sun is but a morning star," can be seen as an attempt to "keep the New World *new*" (15 October 1859, *Journal*). In tramping this perpetual journey, Thoreau embodies a vision of education that is never completed, always vibrantly alive to the immediate circumstances of life.

Indeed, if we keep in mind this sense of education as a process, a never-ending cycle or spiral, we can see the underlying coherence of Thoreau's statements behind the apparent contradictions—his scorn of pedantry and his love of classics, his injunctions to live in the now and his concern for history, his allegiance to nature and his commitment to human culture. Just as Emerson sees learning as an undulating, rhythmic motion—"the mind now thinks, now acts" (*Essays*, 62) — Thoreau writes, equally rhythmically, "We have our times of action and our times of reflection," either of which alone soon becomes meaningless or sterile. Thoreau can praise the activity of reading extravagantly, as he does in the sections included here from "Reading," and then begin the next chapter, "But while we are confined to books . . . we are in danger of forgetting the language which all things and events speak without metaphor" (*Walden*, 111). Even within a single sentence Thoreau expresses the paradoxical interactions between knowing and unknowing, learning and unlearning: "At the same time that we are earnest to explore and learn all things, we require that all things be mysterious and unexplorable, that land and sea be infinitely wild, unsurveyed and unfathomed by us because unfathomable." Any learning, any cultural construction, can be only what Robert Frost called "a momentary stay against confusion."

While Thoreau sees this cycle as at the heart of the entire educational process, it is in the area of writing, of language-making, that he writes with the greatest depth and specificity. This is the learning activity he himself engaged in daily, noting: "How vain it is to sit down to write when you have not stood up to live!" (19 August 1851, *Journal*). Emerson, who first encouraged Thoreau to keep a journal, had noted in *Nature* (1836) a kind of linguistic entropy that results when language loses touch with the physicality from which it arose, becoming fossilized through habit and increasing abstraction. To counteract this force, the true American scholar must "pierce this rotten diction and fasten words again to visible things" (*Essays*, 23). Or, as Thoreau puts it, playing on the etymology of the word *parlor* as relating to speech, "It would seem as if the very *language* of our parlors would lose all its nerve and degenerate into *palaver* wholly, our lives pass at such remoteness from its symbols, and its metaphors and tropes are necessarily so far fetched, through slides and dumb-waiters, as it were; in other words, the parlor is so far from the kitchen and workshop" (*Walden,* 245). The writer who uses only the existing language is a secondary or derivative one, not a "maker" but an imitator; the true writer—and learner— must move beyond the prison-house of language to construct new forms more responsive to the immediate time, helping us see what previous forms left out. As Thoreau writes, he illustrates his point by using concrete sensory metaphors: "He would be a poet who could impress the winds and streams into his service, to speak for him; who nailed words to their primitive senses, as farmers drive down stakes in the spring, which the frost has heaved; who derived his words as often as he used them,—transplanted them to his page with earth adhering to their roots" (*Natural History Essays,* 120). The writer reembodies language not only by heeding outside nature but by writing from his entire physical existence, from "thoughts which the body thought" (9 November 1851, *Journal*); "We reason from our hands to our head" (5 September 1851, *Journal*). Elsewhere, he writes: "The forcible writer stands bodily behind his words with his experience—He does not make books out of books, but he has been *there* in person" (3 February 1852, *Journal*), anticipating the words of one of Zora Neale Hurston's characters: "You got tuh go there tuh know there."

So when Thoreau retreats to Walden Pond or takes

one of his shorter excursions to wilder places like the Maine woods, it is not to commune mutely with "nature" but to explore and exploit sources for new language, which is also new knowledge. He hoes beans, he tells us, not for food or trade but "for the sake of tropes and expressions, to serve a parable-maker one day" (*Walden*, 162). Some progressive educators make the mistake of thinking it is enough for students to have experiences, but experiences are educative only if the students actively clarify, internalize, and reflect on them through their own language-making. The corresponding mistake of educational conservatives is to assume that inert bits and pieces of culture committed to memory somehow constitute thinking. It is one of the many ironies of our current schooling that Thoreau's writings themselves have become fodder for mindless exam questions instead of the "perpetual suggestions and provocations" (*Walden*, 100) he sought from his own reading; we should not so much venerate and memorialize Thoreau's writing as use it to spur our own: "Thought breeds thought. It grows under your hands" (13 February 1860, *Journal*).

And indeed it is the energy, the provocativeness, of Thoreau's writings on education that is his crucial legacy to us as learners, parents, and teachers. If Thoreau was not as original in his teaching practice as Alcott nor in his reconceptualizing of education as Emerson, he often created a richer, more relevant, and supple language in which to talk about learning and teaching. His embrace of the concrete, his breaking down of dead, abstract language through etymologies and puns, his playful, often apothegmatical wit—such as his critique of external reward: "Let every sheep keep but his own skin" (*Corre-*

spondence, 190) — are the essence both in idea and em-
bodiment of the tradition of the active mind: "The
volatile truth of our words should continually betray the
inadequacy of the residual statement. Their truth is instantly *translated*; its literal monument alone remains"
(*Walden*, 310).

How, then, should we read this book? On the one
hand, we cannot take these excerpts as literal prescrip-
tions even if we could get beyond their apparent contra-
dictoriness. As Thoreau says: "I would not have any one
adopt *my* mode of living on any account; for beside that
before he has fairly learned it I may have found out another for myself. I desire that there may be as many different persons in the world as possible; but I would have
each one be very careful to find out and pursue *his own*
way, and not his father's or his mother's or his neighbor's
instead" (*Walden*, 71). But on the other hand, we cannot
merely let this be a reading and thinking experience
locked away within the mind only. Thoreau said of what
he considered a truly good book: "I must lay it down and
commence living on its hint. . . . What I began by reading
I must finish by acting" (19 February 1841, *Journal*). This
present book exists only to be realized in radically recon-
ceiving and restructuring our schools. If the ideas and
stances here seem visionary, seem like castles in the air,
we must, to use one of Thoreau's metaphors, put the
foundations of reflective action and community-building
under them. The schooling of our children is too crucial
and too exciting to be left to large bureaucracies, professors of education, or top-down quick fixes. As George
Dennison has written, "To be open to experience means,
too, that we cannot repeat past successes with past tech-

niques. We cannot organize the educational event in advance. Certainly we can plan and prepare, but we cannot organize it until we are in it and the students themselves have brought their unique contributions. And so there is a point beyond which our tendency to organize becomes inimical to experience, inimical to teaching" (*The Lives of Children,* 258). Nothing can substitute for the steady, constant application of intelligence and love. As Thoreau says, "No method nor discipline can supersede the necessity of being forever on the alert" (*Walden,* 111).

To avoid overorganizing Thoreau's own thinking, the selections here follow neither chronology nor a strictly topical and segmented structure. Thoreau's faithfulness in following the twists and turns of the immediate thought often leads him to make statements that contradict each other within the total body of his work. However, there is an underlying coherence beneath his shifts and inconsistencies. The structure of this volume is more suggestive and associative than strictly logical, more recursive and spiraling than linearly sequential. It invites the reader to make her or his own kinds of orders and relations among the passages, to actively connect the dots in a personal gestalt of learning and education.

The book begins with a series of passages emphasizing the need to awaken ourselves from abstractions and preconceptions in order to see and learn anew. This strategy is helpful not only for learning in general but for following Thoreau's iconoclastic mind, here working on the subject of education. Then follows a plea for "uncommon schools," where thinking and doing are reunited. Subsequent passages focus more specifically on reading, which Thoreau views not as a prescribed exercise in cultural literacy but as a series of goads to further thinking. The study of books, of course, has to be supplemented, qualified, and contradicted by the direct experience of a life in nature, which is the focus of the next sequence. And this experience of nature must in turn be transformed and reconstructed into a new culture, the task of the arts and sciences, so the following selections are more specifically concerned with learning and creating various disciplines, such as science and history. The volume closes with meditations on the subject in which Thoreau shone the brightest, the learning and teaching of language and writing. The very last passage, from *Walden*, is a plea to the reader to move these words off the page and use them "to solve some of the problems of life, not only theoretically, but practically."

Uncommon Learning

———

THOREAU ON EDUCATION

It is a surprising and memorable, as well as valuable experience, to be lost in the woods any time. Often in a snow storm, even by day, one will come out upon a well-known road, and yet find it impossible to tell which way leads to the village. Though he knows that he has travelled it a thousand times, he cannot recognize a feature in it, but it is as strange to him as if it were a road in Siberia. By night, of course, the perplexity is infinitely greater. In our most trivial walks, we are constantly, though unconsciously, steering like pilots by certain well-known beacons and headlands, and if we go beyond our usual course we still carry in our minds the bearing of some neighboring cape; and not till we are completely lost, or turned round, — for a man needs only to be turned round once with his eyes shut in this world to be lost, — do we appreciate the vastness and strangeness of Nature. Every man has to learn the points of the compass again as often as he awakes, whether from sleep or any abstraction. Not till we are lost, in other words, not till we have lost the world, do we begin to find ourselves, and realize where we are and the infinite extent of our relations.

"The Village," *Walden*, 170–71

Most men even in this comparatively free country, through mere ignorance and mistake, are so occupied with the factitious cares and superfluously coarse labors of life that its finer fruits cannot be plucked by them. Their fingers, from excessive toil, are too clumsy and tremble too much for that. Actually the laboring man has not leisure for a true integrity day by day; he cannot afford to sustain the manliest relations to men; his labor would be depreciated in the market. He has no time to be anything but a machine. How can he remember well his ignorance — which his growth requires — who has so often to use his knowledge?

"Economy," *Walden*, 6

It is only when we forget all our learning that we begin to know. I do not get nearer by a hair's breadth to any natural object so long as I presume that I have an introduction to it from some learned man. To conceive of it with a total apprehension I must for the thousandth time approach it as something totally strange. If you would make acquaintance with the ferns you must forget your botany. You must get rid of what is commonly called *knowledge* of them. Not a single scientific term or distinction is the least to the purpose, for you would fain perceive something, and you must approach the object totally unprejudiced. You must be aware that *no thing* is what you have taken it to be. In what book is this world and its beauty described? Who has plotted the steps toward the discovery of beauty? You have got to be in a different state from common. Your greatest success will be simply to perceive that such things are, and you will have no communication to make to the Royal Society. If it were required to know the position of the fruit-dots or the character of the indusium, nothing could be easier than to ascertain it; but if it is required that you be affected by ferns, that they amount to anything, signify anything, to you, helping to redeem your life, this end is not so surely accomplished. In the one case, you take a sentence and analyze it, you decide if it is printed in large primer or small pica; if it is long or short, simple or compound, and how many clauses it is composed of; if the i's are all dotted, or some for variety without dots; what color and composition of the ink and the paper; and it is considered a fair or mediocre sentence accordingly, and you assign its place among the sentences you have seen and kept specimens of. But as for the meaning of the sentence, that is as completely overlooked as if it had none. This is the Chinese, the Aristotelean, method. But if you should ever perceive the meaning you would disregard all the rest. So far science goes, and it punctually leaves off there, — tells you finally where it is to be found and its synonyms, and rests from its labors.

4 October 1859, *Journal* XII: 371–72

If you would be wise learn science & then forget it.

22 April 1852, *Journal* 4: 483

I have heard that there is a Society for the Diffusion of Useful Knowledge — It is said that Knowledge is power and the like — Methinks there is equal need of a society for the diffusion of useful Ignorance — for what is most of our boasted so called knowledge but a conceit that we know something which robs us of the advantages of our actual ignorance — ... For a man's ignorance sometimes is not only useful but beautiful while his knowledge is of-tentimes worse than useless, beside being ugly.

In reference to important things, whose knowledge amounts to more than a consciousness of his ignorance? Yet what more refreshing & inspiring knowledge than this?

9 February 1851, *Journal* 3: 184

Of two men, one of whom knows nothing about a subject, and what is extremely rare, knows that he knows nothing — and the other really knows something about it, but thinks that he knows all — What great advantage has the latter over the former? Which is the best to deal with?

I do not know that knowledge amounts to anything more definite than a novel & grand surprise on a sudden revelation of the insufficiency of all that we had called knowledge before. An indefinite sense of the grandeur & glory of the Universe. It is the lighting up of the mist by the sun

But man cannot be said to know in any higher sense, than he can look serenely & with impunity in the face of the sun.

27 February 1851, *Journal* 3: 198

When I thought I knew the flowers so well, the beautiful purple azalea or pinxter-flower should be shown me by the hunter who found it. Such facts are lifted quite above the level of the actual. They are all just such events as my imagination prepares me for, no matter how incredible. Perfectly in keeping with my life and characteristic. Ever and anon something will occur which my philosophy has not dreamed of. The limits of the actual are set some thoughts further off. That which had seemed a rigid wall of vast thickness unexpectedly proves a thin and undulating drapery. The boundaries of the actual are no more fixed and rigid than the elasticity of our imaginations. The fact that a rare and beautiful flower which we never saw, perhaps never heard [of], for which therefore there was no place in our thoughts, may at length be found in our immediate neighborhood, is very suggestive.

30 May 1853, *Journal* V: 203–4

As the least drop of wine colors the whole goblet, so the least particle of truth colors our whole life. It is never isolated, or simply added as dollars to our stock. When any real progress is made, we unlearn and learn anew, what we thought we knew before. We go picking up and laying side by side the *disjecta membra* of truth, as he who picked up one by one a row of a hundred stones, and returned with each separately to his basket.

31 December 1838, *Journal* 1: 24–25

My desire for knowledge is intermittent but my desire to commune with the spirit of the universe—to be intoxicated even with the fumes, call it, of that divine nectar—to bear my head through atmospheres and over heights unknown to my feet—is perennial & constant.

It is remarkable how few events or crises there are in our mind's histories—How little *exercised* we have been in our mind—how few experiences we have had. I would fain be assured that I am growing apace & rankly—though.

9 February 1851, *Journal* 3: 185

Knowledge does not come to us by details but by liefer-ungs [sudden revelations] from the gods. What else is it to wash & purify ourselves? Conventionalities are as bad as impurities. Only thought which is expressed by the mind in repose as it were lying on its back & contem-plating the heaven's — is adequately and fully expressed — What are sidelong-transient passing half views? The writer expressing his thought — must be as well seated as the astronomer contemplating the heavens — he must not occupy a constrained position. The facts the experience we are well poised upon — ! Which secures our whole at-tention!

7 July 1851, *Journal* 3: 291

There are nowadays professors of philosophy, but not philosophers. Yet it is admirable to profess because it was once admirable to live. To be a philosopher is not merely to have subtle thoughts, nor even to found a school, but so to love wisdom as to live according to its dictates a life of simplicity, independence, magnanimity, and trust. It is to solve some of the problems of life, not only theoreti-cally, but practically.

"Economy," *Walden*, 14–15

I maintain that the Government ought to provide for the education of all children who would otherwise be brought up, or rather grow up, in ignorance.

In the first place, the welfare of the individual, and in the second that of the community, demand it. It is as much the duty of the parent to educate, as it is to feed and clothe the child. For on what, I would ask, depends this last duty? Why is the child to be fed and clothed, if not to enable him to receive and make a proper use of — an education? an education which he is no better able to obtain for himself, than he is to supply his physical wants. Indeed the culture of the physical is important only so far as it is subservient to that of the intellectual man. No one disputes this. Should then poverty or neglect threaten to rob the child of this right — a right more dear and more worthy to be cherished and defended than any he can enjoy — in such a case, it appears to me to be the duty of that neighbor whose circumstances will allow of it, to *take* the part of the child, and *act* the part of a parent. The duty in this instance amounts to a moral obligation, and is as much a duty to preserve the life of the infant whose unnatural parents would suffer it to starve by the roadside. What can it profit a man that he hath enough to eat and to drink, and the wherewithal he may be clothed, provided he lose his own soul?

But as these wealthy neighbors can accomplish more good by acting in concert, can more effectually relieve the unfortunate by a community of good offices, it is their duty, or, in other words, the duty of the community so to do.

Early Essays and Miscellanies, 60–61

At Cambridge College the mere rent of a student's room, which is only a little larger than my own, is thirty dollars each year, though the corporation had the advantage of building thirty-two side by side and under one roof, and the occupant suffers the inconvenience of many and noisy neighbors, and perhaps a residence in the fourth story. I cannot but think that if only we had more true wisdom in these respects, not only less education would be needed, because, forsooth, more would already have been acquired, but the pecuniary expense of getting an education would in a great measure vanish. Those conveniences which the student requires at Cambridge or elsewhere cost him or somebody else ten times as great a sacrifice of life as they would with proper management on both sides. Those things for which the most money is demanded are never the things which the student most wants. Tuition, for instance, is an important item in the term bill, while for the far more valuable education which he gets by associating with the most cultivated of his contemporaries no charge is made. The mode of founding a college is, commonly, to get up a subscription of dollars and cents, and then following blindly the principles of a division of labor to its extreme, a principle which should never be followed but with circumspection, — to call in a contractor who makes this a subject of speculation, and he employs Irishmen or other operatives actually to lay the foundations, while the students that are to be are said to be fitting themselves for it; and for these oversights successive generations have to pay. I think that it would be *better than this,* for the students, or those who desire to be benefited by it, even to lay the foundation themselves. The student who secures his coveted leisure and retirement by systematically shirking any labor necessary to man obtains but an ignoble and unprofitable leisure, defrauding himself of the experience which alone can make leisure fruitful. "But," says one, "you do not mean that the students should go to work with their hands instead of their heads?" I do not mean that exactly, but I mean something which he might think a good deal like that; I mean that they should not *play* life, or *study* it merely, while the community supports them at this expensive game, but earnestly *live* it from beginning to end. How could youths better learn to live than by at once trying the experiment of living? Methinks this would exercise their minds as much as mathematics. If I wished a boy to know something about the arts and sciences, for instance, I would not pursue the common course, which is merely to send him into the neighborhood of some professor, where any thing is professed and practised but the art of life;—to survey the world through a telescope or a microscope, and never with his natural eye; to study chemistry, and not learn how his bread is made, or mechanics, and not learn how it is earned. To discover new satellites to Neptune, and not detect the motes in his eyes, or devoured by the monsters that swarm all around him, while contemplating the monsters in a drop of vinegar. Which would have advanced the most at the end of a month,—the boy who made his own jack-knife from the ore which he had dug and smelted, reading as much as would be necessary for this,—or the boy who had attended the lectures on metallurgy at the Institute in the mean while, and had received a Rodgers' penknife from his father? Which would be the most likely to cut his fingers?—To my astonishment I was informed on leaving college that I had studied navigation!—why, if I had taken one turn down the harbor I should have known more about it. Even the *poor* student studies and is taught only *political* economy, while that economy of living which is synonymous with philosophy is not even sincerely professed in our colleges. The consequence is, that while he is reading Adam Smith, Ricardo, and Say, he runs his father in debt irretrievably.

"Economy," *Walden,* 50–52

Had a dispute with Father about the *use* of my making this sugar when I knew it could be done and might have bought sugar cheaper at Holden's. He said it took me from my studies. I said I made it my study; I felt as if I had been to a university.

20 March 1856, *Journal* VIII: 217

I think it would be worth the while to introduce a school of children to such a grove, that they may get an idea of the primitive oaks before they are all gone, instead of hiring botanists to lecture to them when it is too late.

2 November 1860, *Journal* XIV: 210

Little did the fathers of the town anticipate this brilliant success when they caused to be imported from further in the country some straight poles with the tops cut off, which they called sugar maple trees, — and a neighboring merchant's clerk, as I remember, by way of jest planted beans about them. Yet these which were then jestingly called bean-poles are these days far the most beautiful objects noticeable in our streets. They are worth all and more than they have cost, — though one of the selectmen did take the cold which occasioned his death in setting them out, — if only because they have filled the open eyes of children with their rich color so unstintedly so many autumns. We will not ask them to yield us sugar in the spring, while they yield us so fair a prospect in the autumn. Wealth may be the inheritance of few in the houses, but it is equally distributed on the Common. All children alike can revel in this golden harvest. These trees, throughout the street, are at least equal to an annual festival and holiday, or a week of such, — not requiring any special police to keep the peace,—and poor indeed must be that New England village's October, which has not the maple in its streets. This October festival costs no powder nor ringing of bells, but every tree is a liberty-pole on which a thousand bright flags are run up. Hundreds of children's eyes are steadily drinking in this color, and by these teachers even the truants are caught and educated the moment they step abroad. It is as if some cheap and innocent gala-day were celebrated in our town every autumn,—a week or two of such days.

What meant the fathers by establishing this *living* institution before the church,—this institution which needs no repairing nor repainting, which is continually "enlarged and repaired" by its growth? Surely trees should be set in our streets with a view to their October splendor. Do you not think it will make some odds to these children that they were brought up under the maples? Indeed, neither the truant nor the studious are at present taught colors in the schools. These are instead of the bright colors in apothecary shops and city windows. It is a pity we have not more red maples and some hickories in the streets as well. Our paint-box is imperfectly filled. Instead of, or besides, supplying paint-boxes, I would supply these natural colors to the young.

18 October 1858, *Journal* XI: 218–19

With a little more deliberation in the choice of their pursuits, all men would perhaps become essentially students and observers, for certainly their nature and destiny are interesting to all alike. In accumulating property for ourselves and our posterity, in founding a family or a state, or acquiring fame even, we are mortal; but in dealing with truth we are immortal, and need fear no change nor accident. The oldest Egyptian or Hindoo philosopher raised a corner of the veil from the statue of the divinity; and still the trembling robe remains raised, and I gaze upon as fresh a glory as he did, since it was I in him that was then so bold, and it is he in me that now reviews the vision. No dust has settled on that robe; no time has elapsed since that divinity was revealed. That time which we really improve, or which is improvable, is neither past, present nor future.

"Reading," *Walden*, 99

It would be worth the while to select our reading, for books are the society we keep; to read only the serenely true; never statistics, nor fiction, nor news, nor reports, nor periodicals, but only great poems, and when they failed, read them again, or perchance write more. Instead of other sacrifice, we might offer up our perfect thoughts to the gods daily, in hymns or psalms. For we should be at the helm at least once a day. The whole of the day should not be day-time; there should be one hour, if no more, which the day did not bring forth. Scholars are wont to sell their birthright for a mess of learning. But is it necessary to know what the speculator prints, or the thoughtless study, or the idle read, the literature of the Russians and the Chinese, or even French philosophy and much of German criticism. Read the best books first, or you may not have a chance to read them at all.

"Sunday," *A Week on the Concord
and Merrimack Rivers*, 95–96

The student may read Homer or Aeschylus in the Greek without danger of dissipation or luxuriousness, for it implies that he in some measure emulate their heroes, and consecrate morning hours to their pages. The heroic books, even if printed in the character of our mother tongue, will always be in a language dead to degenerate times; and we must laboriously seek the meaning of each word and line, conjecturing a larger sense than common use permits out of what wisdom and valor and generosity we have. The modern cheap and fertile press, with all its translations, has done little to bring us nearer to the heroic writers of antiquity. They seem as solitary, and the letter in which they are printed as rare and curious, as ever. It is worth the expense of youthful days and costly hours, if you learn only some words of an ancient language, which are raised out of the trivialness of the street, to be perpetual suggestions and provocations. It is not in vain that the farmer remembers and repeats the few Latin words which he has heard. Men sometimes speak as if the study of the classics would at length make way for more modern and practical studies; but the adventurous student will always study classics, in whatever language they may be written and however ancient they may be. For what are the classics but the noblest recorded thoughts of man? They are the only oracles which are not decayed, and there are such answers to the most modern inquiry in them as Delphi and Dodona never gave. We might as well omit to study Nature because she is old. To read well, that is, to read true books in a true spirit, is a noble exercise, and one that will task the reader more than any exercise which the customs of the day esteem. It requires a training such as the athletes underwent, the steady intention almost of the whole life to this object. Books must be read as deliberately and reservedly as they were written.

"Reading," *Walden*, 100–101

Certainly, we do not need to be soothed and entertained always like children. He who resorts to the easy novel, because he is languid, does no better than if he took a nap. The front aspect of great thoughts can only be enjoyed by those who stand on the side, whence they arrive. Books, not which afford us a cowering enjoyment, but in which each thought is of unusual daring; such as an idle man cannot read, and a timid one would not be entertained by, which even make us dangerous to existing institutions, — such call I good books.

All that are printed and bound are not books; they do not necessarily belong to letters, but are oftener to be ranked with other luxuries and appendages of civilized life. Base wares are palmed off under a thousand disguises. "The way to trade," as a pedler once told me, "is to *put it right through*," no matter what it is, any thing that is agreed on. —

> "You grov'ling worldling, you whose wisdom trades
> Where light ne'er shot his golden ray."

By dint of able writing and pen-craft, books are cunningly compiled, and have their run and success even among the learned, as if they were the result of a new man's thinking, and their birth were attended with some natural throes. But in a little while their covers fall off, for no binding will avail, and it appears that they are not Books or Bibles at all. There are new and patented inventions in this shape, purporting to be for the elevation of the race, which many a pure scholar and genius who has learned to read is for a moment deceived by, and find himself reading a horse-rake, or spinning jenny, or wooden nutmeg, or oak-leaf cigar, or steam-power press,

or kitchen range, perchance, when he was seeking serene
and biblical truth. —

> "Merchants arise,
> And mingle conscience with your merchandise."

Paper is cheap, and authors need not now erase one book
before they write another. Instead of cultivating the earth
for wheat and potatoes, they cultivate literature, and fill a
place in the Republic of Letters. Or they would fain write
for fame merely, as others actually raise crops of grain to
be distilled into brandy. Books are for the most part wil-
fully and hastily written, as parts of a system, to supply a
want real or imagined. Books of natural history aim commonly to be hasty schedules or inventories of God's
property, by some clerk. They do not in the least teach
the divine view of nature, but the popular view, or rather
the popular method of studying nature, and make haste
to conduct the persevering pupil only into that dilemma
where the professors always dwell —

> "To Athens gown'd he goes, and from that school
> Returns unsped, a more instructed fool."

They teach the elements really of ignorance, not of
knowledge, for to speak deliberately and in view of the
highest truths, it is not easy to distinguish elementary
knowledge. There is a chasm between knowledge and ignorance which the arches of science can never span. A
book should contain pure discoveries, glimpses of *terra
firma,* though by shipwrecked mariners, and not the art
of navigation by those who have never been out of sight
of land. They must not yield wheat and potatoes, but

must themselves be the unconstrained and natural harvest of their author's lives. —

"What I have learned is mine; I've had my thought,
And me the Muses noble truths have taught."

We do not learn much from learned books, but from true, sincere, human books, from frank and honest biographies. The life of a good man will hardly improve us more than the life of a freebooter, for the inevitable laws appear as plainly in the infringement as the observance, and our lives are sustained by a nearly equal expense of virtue of some kind. The decaying tree, while yet it lives demands sun, wind, and rain no less than the green one. It secretes sap and performs the functions of health. If we choose, we may study the alburnum only. The gnarled stump has as tender a bud as the sapling.

At least let us have healthy books, a stout horse-rake or a kitchen range which is not cracked. Let not the poet shed tears only for the public weal. He should be as vigorous as a sugar-maple, with sap enough to maintain his own verdure, beside what runs into the troughs, and not like a vine, which being cut in the spring bears no fruit, but bleeds to death in the endeavor to heal its wounds. The poet is he that hath fat enough, like bears and marmots, to suck his claws all winter.

"Sunday," *A Week on the Concord
and Merrimack Rivers*, 96–99

A book should be so true as to be intimate and familiar to all men — as the sun to their faces. Such a word as is occasionally uttered to a companion in the woods in summer, and both are silent.

4 September 1841, *Journal* 1: 330

Those who have not learned to read the ancient classics in the language in which they were written must have a very imperfect knowledge of the history of the human race; for it is remarkable that no transcript of them has ever been made into any modern tongue, unless our civilization itself may be regarded as such a transcript. Homer has never yet been printed in English, nor Aeschylus, nor Virgil even, — works as refined, as solidly done, and as beautiful almost as the morning itself; for later writers, say what we will of their genius, have rarely, if ever, equalled the elaborate beauty and finish and the lifelong and heroic literary labors of the ancients. They only talk of forgetting them who never knew them. It will be soon enough to forget them when we have the learning and the genius which will enable us to attend and appreciate them. That age will be rich indeed when those relics which we call Classics, and the still older and more than classic but even less known Scriptures of the nations, shall have still further accumulated, when the Vaticans shall be filled with Vedas and Zendavestas and Bibles, with Homers and Dantes and Shakespeares, and all the centuries to come shall have successively deposited their trophies in the forum of the world.

The works of the great poets have never yet been read by mankind, for only great poets can read them. They have only been read as the multitude read the stars, at most astrologically, not astronomically. Most men have learned to read to serve a paltry convenience, as they have learned to cipher in order to keep accounts and not be cheated in trade; but of reading as a noble intellectual exercise they know little or nothing; yet this only is reading, in a high sense, not that which lulls us as a luxury and suffers the nobler faculties to sleep the while, but what we have to stand on tiptoe to read and devote our most alert and wakeful hours to.

"Reading," *Walden*, 103–4

I have sometimes imagined a library i.e. a collection of the works of true poets philosophers naturalists & c deposited not in a brick or marble edifice in a crowded and dusty city — guarded by cold-blooded & methodical officials — & preyed on by bookworms — In which you own no share, and are not likely to — but rather far away in the depths of a primitive forest — like the ruins of central American alcoves — the older books protecting the more modern from the elements — partially buried by the luxuriance of nature — which the heroic student could reach only after adventures in the wilderness, amid wild beasts & wild men — That to my imagination seems a fitter place for these interesting relics, which owe no small part of their interest to their antiquity — and whose occasion is nature — than the well preserved edifice — with its well preserved officials on the side of a city's square.

3 February 1852, *Journal* 4: 321–23

A truly good book attracts very little favor of itself — It is so true that it teaches me better to read it — I must soon lay it down and commence living on its hint — I do not see how any can be written more, but this is the last effusion of genius.

When I read an indifferent book — it seems the best thing I can do, but the inspiring volume hardly leaves me leisure to finish its latter pages — It is slipping out of my fingers while I read. It creates no atmosphere in which it may be perused, but one in which its teaching may be practiced — It confers on me no such wealth that I lay it down with the least regret — What I began by reading I must finish by acting.

— So I cannot stay to hear a *good* sermon and applaud at the conclusion, but I shall be half-way to Thermopylae before that.

19 February 1841, *Journal* 1: 268

But while we are confined to books, though the most select and classic, and read only particular written languages, which are themselves but dialects and provincial, we are in danger of forgetting the language which all things and events speak without metaphor, which alone is copious and standard. Much is published, but little printed. The rays which stream through the shutter will be no longer remembered when the shutter is wholly removed. No method nor discipline can supersede the necessity of being forever on the alert. What is a course of history, or philosophy, or poetry, no matter how well selected, or the best society, or the most admirable routine of life, compared with the discipline of looking always at what is to be seen? Will you be a reader, a student merely, or a seer? Read your fate, see what is before you, and walk on into futurity.

"Sounds," *Walden*, 111

I think that having learned our letters we should read the best that is in literature and not be forever repeating our a b abs, and words of one syllable, in the fourth or fifth classes, sitting on the lowest and foremost form all our lives. Most men are satisfied if they read or hear read, and perchance have been convicted by the wisdom of one

good book, the Bible, and for the rest of their lives vegetate and dissipate their faculties in what is called easy
reading. There is a work in several volumes in our Circulating Library entitled Little Reading, which I thought
referred to a town of that name which I had not been to.
There are those who, like cormorants and ostriches, can
digest all sorts of this, even after the fullest dinner of
meats and vegetables, for they suffer nothing to be
wasted. If others are the machines to provide this provender, they are the machines to read it. They read the nine
thousandth tale about Zebulon and Sephronia, and how
they loved as none had ever loved before, and neither did
the course of their true love run smooth,—at any rate,
how it did run and stumble, and get up again and go on!
how some poor unfortunate got up into a steeple, who
had better never have gone up as far as the belfry; and
then, having needlessly got him up there, the happy novelist rings the bell for all the world to come together and
hear, O dear! how he did get down again! For my part, I
think that they had better metamorphose all such aspiring heroes of universal noveldom into man weathercocks, as they used to put heroes among the constellations, and let them swing round there till they are rusty,
and not come down at all to bother honest men with their
pranks.

"Reading," *Walden*, 104–5

It is necessary to find out exactly what books to read on
a given subject—Though there may be a thousand
books written upon it, it is only important to read 3 or 4
—they will contain all that is essential—& a few pages
will show which they are. Books which are books are all

that you want—& there are but half a dozen in any thousand. I saw that while we are clearing the forest in our westward progress we are accumulating a forest of books in our rear—as wild & unexplored as any of nature's primitive wildernesses.

16 March 1852, *Journal* 4: 392

The best books are not read even by those who are called good readers. What does our Concord culture amount to? There is in this town, with very few exceptions, no taste for the best or for very good books, even in English literature, whose words all can read and spell. Even the college-bred and so called liberally educated men here and elsewhere have really little or no acquaintance with the English classics; and as for the recorded wisdom of mankind, the ancient classics and Bibles, which are accessible to all who will know of them, there are the feeblest efforts any where to become acquainted with them. I know a woodchopper, of middle age, who takes a French paper, not for news as he says, for he is above that, but to "keep himself in practice," he being a Canadian by birth; and when I ask him what he considers the best thing he can do in this world, he says, beside this, to keep up and add to his English. This is about as much as the college bred generally do or aspire to do, and they take an English paper for the purpose. One who has just come from reading perhaps one of the best English books will find how many with whom he can converse about it? Or suppose he comes from reading a Greek or Latin classic in the original, whose praises are familiar even to the so called illiterate; he will find nobody at all to speak to, but must keep silence about it. Indeed, there is hardly the professor in our colleges, who, if he has mastered the difficulties of the language, has proportionally mastered the difficulties of the wit and poetry of a Greek poet, and has any sympathy to impart to the alert and heroic reader; and as for the sacred Scriptures, or Bibles of mankind, who in this town can tell me even their titles? Most men do not know that any nation but the Hebrews have had a scripture. A man, any man, will go considerably out of his way to pick up a silver dollar; but here are golden words, which the wisest of antiquity have uttered, and whose worth the wise of every succeeding age have assured us of;—and yet we learn to read only as far as Easy Reading, the primers and class-books, and when we leave school, the "Little Reading," and story books, which are for boys and beginners; and our reading, our conversation and thinking, are all on a very low level, worthy only of pygmies and manikins.

"Reading," *Walden*, 106–7

We are under-bred and low-lived and illiterate; and in this respect, I confess I do not make any very broad distinction between the illiterateness of my townsman who cannot read at all, and the illiterateness of him who has learned to read only what is for children and feeble intellects. We should be as good as the worthies of antiquity, but partly by first knowing how good they were. We are a race of tit-men, and soar but little higher in our intellectual flights than the columns of the daily paper.

It is not all books that are as dull as their readers. There are probably words addressed to our condition exactly, which, if we could really hear and understand, would be more salutary than the morning or the spring to our lives, and possibly put a new aspect on the face of things for us. How many a man has dated a new era in his life from the reading of a book. The book exists for us perchance which will explain our miracles and reveal new ones. The at present unutterable things we may find somewhere uttered. These same questions that disturb and puzzle and confound us have in their turn occurred to all the wise men; not one has been omitted; and each has answered them according to his ability, by his words and his life. Moreover, with wisdom we shall learn liberality. The solitary hired man on a farm in the outskirts of Concord, who has had his second birth and peculiar religious exclusiveness by his faith, may think it is not true; but Zoroaster, thousands of years ago, travelled the same road and had the same experience; but he, being wise, knew it to be universal, and treated his neighbors accordingly, and is even said to have invented and established worship among men. Let him humbly commune with Zoroaster, then, and through the liberalizing influence of all the worthies, with Jesus Christ himself, and let "our church" go by the board.

"Reading," *Walden*, 107–8

No face which we can give to a matter will stead us so well at last as the truth. This alone wears well. For the most part, we are not where we are, but in a false position. . . . In sane moments we regard only the facts, the case that is. Say what you have to say, not what you ought. Any truth is better than make-believe. Tom Hyde, the tinker, standing on the gallows, was asked if he had any thing to say. "Tell the tailors," said he, "to remember to make a knot in their thread before they take the first stitch." His companion's prayer is forgotten.

"Conclusion," *Walden,* 327–28

We of Massachusetts boast a good deal of what we do for the education of our people — of our district-school system — & yet our district schools are as it were but infant schools — & we have no system for the education of the great mass who are grown up. — I have yet to learn that one cent is spent by this town — this political community called Concord directly to educate the great mass of its inhabitants who have long since left the district school.

27 September 1851, *Journal* 4: 101

We boast that we belong to the nineteenth century and are making the most rapid strides of any nation. But consider how little this village does for its own culture. I do not wish to flatter my townsmen, nor be flattered by them, for that will not advance either of us. We need to be provoked, — goaded like oxen, as we are, into a trot. We have a comparatively decent system of common schools, schools for infants only; but excepting the half-starved Lyceum in the winter, and laterly the puny beginning of a library suggested by the state, no school for ourselves. We spend more on almost any article of bodily aliment or ailment than on our mental aliment. It is time that we had uncommon schools, that we did not leave off our education when we begin to be men and women. It is time that villages were universities, and their elder inhabitants the fellows of universities, with leisure — if they are indeed so well off — to pursue liberal studies the rest of their lives.

Shall the world be confined to one Paris or one Oxford forever? Cannot students be boarded here and get a liberal education under the skies of Concord? Can we not hire some Abelard to lecture to us? Alas! what with foddering the cattle and tending the store, we are kept from school too long, and our education is sadly neglected. In this country, the village should in some respects take the place of the nobleman of Europe. It should be the patron of the fine arts. It is rich enough. It wants only the magnanimity and refinement. It can spend money enough on such things as farmers and traders value, but it is thought Utopian to propose spending money for things which more intelligent men know to be of far more worth. This town has spent seventeen thousand dollars on a townhouse, thank fortune or politics, but it will not spend so much on living wit, the true meat to put into that shell, in a hundred years. The one hundred and twenty-five dollars annually subscribed for a Lyceum in the winter is better spent than any other equal sum raised in the town. If we live in the nineteenth century, why should we not enjoy the advantages which the nineteenth century offers? If we read newspapers, why not skip the gossip of Boston and take the best newspaper in the world at once? — not be sucking the pap of "neutral family" papers, or browsing "Olive-Branches" here in New England. Let the reports of all the learned societies come to us, and we will see if they know anything. Why should we leave it to Harper & Brothers and Redding & Co. to select our reading? As the nobleman of cultivated taste surrounds himself with whatever conduces to his culture, — genius — learning — wit — books — paintings — statuary — music — philosophical instruments, and the like; so let the village do, — not stop short at a pedagogue, a parson, a sexton, a parish library, and three selectmen, because our pilgrim forefathers got through a cold winter once on a bleak rock with these. To act collectively is according to the spirit of our institutions; and I am confident that, as our circumstances are more flourishing, our means are greater than the nobleman's. New England can hire all the wise men in the world to come and teach her, and board them round the while, and not be provincial at all. That is the *uncommon* school we want. Instead of noblemen, let us have noble villages of men. If it is necessary, omit one bridge over the river, go round a little there, and throw one arch at least over the darker gulf of ignorance which surrounds us.

"Reading," *Walden*, 108–10

Solitude is not measured by the miles of space that intervene between a man and his fellows. The really diligent student in one of the crowded hives of Cambridge College is as solitary as a dervish in the desert. The farmer can work alone in the fields or the woods all day, hoeing or chopping, and not feel lonesome, because he is employed; but when he comes home at night he cannot sit down in a room alone, at the mercy of his thoughts, but must be where he can "see the folks," and recreate, and as he thinks remunerate himself for his day's solitude; and hence he wonders how the student can sit alone in the house all night and most of the day without ennui and "the blues;" but he does not realize that the student, though in the house, is still at work in *his* field, and chopping in *his* woods, and the farmer in his, and in turn seeks the same recreation and society that the latter does, though it may be a more condensed form of it.

"Solitude," *Walden*, 135–36

We seem to have forgotten that the expression, a *liberal* education, originally meant among the Romans one worthy of *free* men; while the learning of trades and professions by which to get your livelihood merely, was considered worthy of *slaves* only. But taking a hint from the word, I would go a step further and say, that it is not the man of wealth and leisure simply, though devoted to art, or science, or literature, who, in a true sense is *liberally* educated but only the earnest and *free* man. In a slave-holding country like this, there can be no such thing as *liberal* education tolerated by the State; and those scholars of Austria and France who, however learned they may be, are contented under their tyrannies, have received only a *servile* education.

"The Last Days of John Brown," *Reform Papers*, 151

Don't spend your time in drilling soldiers, who may turn out hirelings after all, but give to undrilled peasantry a *country* to fight for. The schools begin with what they call elements, and where do they end?

Letter to H. G. O. Blake, 26 September 1855,
Correspondence, 384

Many go to Europe *to finish their education,* and when they have returned their friends remark that the most they have acquired is a correct pronunciation of English. It is a premature hardening but hollowing of the shell. They become valuable utensils of the gourd kind, but

have no palatable and nutritious inside. Instead of acquiring nutritious and palatable qualities to their pulp, it
is all absorbed into a prematurely hardened shell. They
went away squashes, and they return gourds. They are all
expressed, or squeezed out; their essential oil is gone.
They are pronounced for you; they are good to stand before or for a noun or man as handles; not even hollow
gourds always, but the handle without the mug. They
pronounce with the sharp precise report of a rifle, but the
likeness is in the sound only, for they have no bullets to
fire.

30 July 1853, Journal V: 344–45

Goethe's whole education and life were those of the
artist. He lacks the unconsciousness of the poet. In his
autobiography he describes accurately the life of the author of Wilhelm Meister. For as there is in that book, min-
gled with a rare and serene wisdom, a certain pettiness or
exaggeration of trifles, wisdom applied to produce a constrained and partial and merely well-bred man, — a mag-
nifying of the theatre till life itself is turned into a stage,
for which it is our duty to study our parts well, and conduct with propriety and precision, — so in the autobiography, the fault of his education is, so to speak, its merely
artistic completeness. Nature is hindered, though she
prevails at last in making an unusually catholic impres-
sion on the boy. It is the life of a city boy, whose toys are
pictures and works of art, whose wonders are the theatre
and kingly processions and crownings. As the youth
studied minutely the order and the degrees in the imper-
ial procession, and suffered none of its effect to be lost on
him; so the man aimed to secure a rank in society which

would satisfy his notion of fitness and respectability. He was defrauded of much which the savage boy enjoys. Indeed he himself has occasion to say in this very autobiography, when at last he escapes into the woods without the gates, — "Thus much is certain, that only the undefinable, wide-expanding feelings of youth and of uncultivated nations are adapted to the sublime, which, whenever it may be excited in us through external objects, since it is either formless, or else moulded into forms which are incomprehensible, must surround us with a grandeur which we find above our reach." He further says of himself, — "I had lived among painters from my childhood, and had accustomed myself to look at objects, as they did, with reference to art." And this was his practice to the last. He was even too *well-bred* to be thoroughly bred. He says that he had had no intercourse with the lowest class of his towns-boys. The child should have the advantage of ignorance as well as of knowledge, and is fortunate if he gets his share of neglect and exposure.

"Thursday," *A Week on the Concord and Merrimack Rivers*, 327–28

Perhaps I should give some account of myself. I would make education a pleasant thing both to the teacher and the scholar. This discipline, which we allow to be the end of life, should not be one thing in the schoolroom, and another in the street. We should seek to be fellow students with the pupil, and should learn of, as well as with him, if we would be most helpful to him. But I am not blind to the difficulties of the case; it supposes a degree of freedom which rarely exists. It hath not entered into the heart of man to conceive the full import of that word

—Freedom—not a paltry Republican freedom, with a *posse comitatus* at his heels to administer it in doses as to a sick child—but a freedom proportionate to the dignity of his nature—a freedom that shall make him feel that he is a man among men, and responsible only to that Reason of which he is a particle, for his thoughts and his actions.

I have even been disposed to regard the cowhide as a nonconductor. Methinks that, unlike the electric wire, not a single spark of truth is ever transmitted through its agency to the slumbering intellect it would address. I mistake, it may teach a truth in physics, but never a truth in morals.

Letter to Orestes Brownson, 30 December 1837,
Correspondence, 20

What I was learning in college was chiefly, I think, to express myself, and I see now, that as the old orator prescribed, 1st action; 2d, action; 3d action; my teachers should have prescribed, 1st, sincerity; 2d, sincerity; 3d sincerity. The old mythology is incomplete, without a god or goddess of sincerity, on whose altars we might offer up all the products of our farms, our workshops, and our studies.

Letter to Richard Fuller, 2 April 1843,
Correspondence, 93

I require of any lecturer that he will read me a more or less simple and sincere account of his own life, of what he has done and thought,—not so much what he has read or heard of other men's lives and actions, but some such account as he would send to his kindred from a distant land,—and if he has lived sincerely, it must have been in a distant land to me, — describing even his outward circumstances and what adventures he has had, as well as his thoughts and feelings about them. He who gives us only the results of other men's lives, though with brilliant temporary success, we may in some measure justly accuse of having defrauded us of our time. We want him to give us that which was most precious to him, — not his life's blood but even that for which his life's blood circulated, what he has got by living. If anything ever yielded him pure pleasure or instruction, let him communicate it. Let the money-getter tell us how much he loves wealth, and what means he takes to accumulate it. He must describe those facts which he knows and loves better than anybody else. He must not write on foreign missions. The mechanic will naturally lecture about his trade, the farmer about his farm, and every man about that which he, compared with other men, knows best. Yet incredible mistakes are made. I have heard an owl lecture with perverse show of learning upon the solar microscope, and chanticleer upon nebulous stars, when both ought to have been sound asleep, the one in a hollow tree, the other on his roost.

After I lectured here before, this winter, I heard that some of my townsmen had expected of me some account of my life at the pond. This I will endeavor to give tonight.

1837–47, Journal I: 484–85

In most books, the *I*, or first person, is omitted; in this it will be retained; that, in respect to egotism, is the main difference. We commonly do not remember that it is, after all, always the first person that is speaking. I should not talk so much about myself if there were any body else whom I knew as well. Unfortunately, I am confined to this theme by the narrowness of my experience.

"Economy," *Walden*, 3

It is strange that men are in such haste to get fame as teachers rather than knowledge as learners.

10 March 1856, *Journal* XIV: 205

I am still a learner, not a teacher, feeding somewhat omnivorously, browsing both stalk & leaves—but I shall perhaps be enabled to speak with the more precision & authority by & by—if philosophy & sentiment are not buried under a multitude of details.

Letter to H. G. O. Blake, 21 May 1856,
Correspondence, 423–24

It is the highest compliment to suppose that in the intervals of conversation your companion has expanded and grown—It may be a deference which he will not understand, but the nature which underlies him will understand it—and your influence will be shed as finely on him as the dust in the sun settles on our clothes. By such politeness we may educate one another to some purpose. So have I felt myself educated sometimes—I am expanded and enlarged.

29 April 1841, *Journal* 1: 306

With a certain wariness, but not without a slight shudder at the danger oftentimes, I perceive how near I had come to admitting into my mind details of some trivial affair, as a case at court—And I am astonished to observe how

willing men are to lumber their minds with such rubbish
—to permit idle rumors tales incidents even of an insignificant kind—to intrude upon what should be the sacred ground of the thoughts Shall the temple of our
thought be a public arena where the most trivial affair of
the market & the gossip of the teatable is discussed—a
dusty noisy trivial place—or shall it be a quarter of
heaven itself—a place consecrated to the service of the
gods—a hypaethral temple. I find it so difficult to dis-
pose of the few facts which to me are significant that I
hesitate to burden my mind with the most insignificant
which only a divine mind could illustrate. Such is for the
most part the news—in newspapers & conversation. It is
important to preserve the mind's chastity in this respect.
Think of admitting the details of a single case at the crim-
inal court into the mind—to stalk profanely through its
very sanctum sanctorum for an hour—aye for many
hours—to make a very bar-room of your mind's inmost
apartment—as if for a moment the dust of the street had
occupied you—aye the very street itself with all its travel
passed through your very mind of minds—your
thoughts shrine with all its filth & bustle—Would it not
be an intellectual suicide? By all manner of boards &
traps threatening the extreme penalty of the divine law
excluding trespassers from these grounds it behooves us
to preserve the purity & sanctity of the mind. It is hard to
forget what it is worse than useless to remember. If I am
to be a channel or thorough—I prefer that it be of the
mountain springs—& not the town sewers—The Par-
nassian streams There is inspiration—the divine gossip
which comes to the ear of the attentive mind—from the
Courts of Heaven—there is the profane & stale revela-

tion of the barroom & the police Court. The same ear is fitted to receive both communications—only the character of the individual determines to which source chiefly it shall be open & to which closed. I believe that the mind can be profaned by the habit of attending to trivial things so that all our thoughts shall be tinged with triviality. They shall be dusty as stones in the street—Our very minds shall be paved and macadamized as it were—their foundation broken into fragments for the wheels of travel to roll over. If we have thus desecrated ourselves the remedy will be by circumspection—& wariness by our aspiration & devotion, to consecrate ourselves—to make a fane of the mind. I think that we should treat ourselves as innocent & ingenuous children whose guardians we are —be careful what objects & what subjects we thrust on its attention.

Even the facts of science may dust the mind by their dryness—unless they are in a sense effaced each morning or rather rendered fertile by the dews of fresh & living truth. Every thought that passes through the mind helps to wear & tear it & to deepen the ruts which as in the streets of Pompeii evince how much it has been used. How many things there are concerning which we might well deliberate whether we had better know them. Routine—conventionality manners & c & c—how insensibly and undue attention to these dissipates & impoverishes the mind—robs it of its simplicity and strength emasculates it.

7 July 1851, *Journal* 3: 289–91

I left the woods for as good a reason as I went there. Perhaps it seemed to me that I had several more lives to live, and could not spare any more time for that one. It is remarkable how easily and insensibly we fall into a particular route, and make a beaten track for ourselves. I had not lived there a week before my feet wore a path from my door to the pond-side; and though it is five or six years since I trod it, it is still quite distinct. It is true, I fear that others may have fallen into it, and so helped to keep it open. The surface of the earth is soft and impressible by the feet of men; and so with the paths which the mind travels. How worn and dusty, then, must be the highways of the world, how deep the ruts of tradition and conformity!

"Conclusion," *Walden*, 323

Always you have to contend with the stupidity of men. It is like a stiff soil, a hard-pan. If you go deeper than usual, you are sure to meet with a pan made harder even by the superficial cultivation. The stupid you have always with you. Men are more obedient at first to words than ideas. They mind names more than things. Read to them a lecture on "Education," naming that subject, and they will think that they have heard something important, but call it "Transcendentalism," and they will think it moonshine. Or halve your lecture, and put a psalm at the beginning and a prayer at the end of it and read it from a pulpit, and they will pronounce it good without thinking.

13 February 1860, *Journal* XIII: 145

When some rare northern bird like the pine grosbeak is seen thus far south in the winter, he does not suggest poverty, but dazzles us with his beauty. There is in them a warmth akin to the warmth that melts the icicle. Think of these brilliant, warm-colored, and richly warbling birds, birds of paradise, dainty-footed, downy-clad, in the midst of a New England, a Canadian winter. The woods and fields now somewhat solitary, being deserted by their more tender summer residents, are now frequented by these rich but delicately tinted and hardy northern immigrants of the air. Here is no imperfection to be suggested. The winter, with its snow and ice, is not an evil to be corrected. It is as it was designed and made to be, for the artist has had leisure to add beauty to use. My acquaintances, angels from the north. I had a vision thus prospectively of these birds as I stood in the swamps. I saw this familiar—too *familiar*—fact at a different angle, and I was charmed and haunted by it. But I could only attain to be thrilled and enchanted, as by the sound of a strain of music dying away. I had seen into paradisaic regions, with their air and sky, and I was no longer wholly or merely a denizen of this vulgar earth. Yet had I hardly a foothold there. I was only sure that I was charmed and no mistake. It is only necessary to behold thus the least fact or phenomenon, however familiar, from a point a hair's breadth aside from our habitual routine, to be overcome, enchanted by its beauty and significance. Only what we have touched and worn is trivial,— our scurf, repetition, tradition, conformity. To perceive freshly, with fresh senses, is to be inspired. Great winter itself looked like a precious gem, reflecting rainbow colors from one angle.

11 December 1855, *Journal* VIII: 43–44

How much virtue there is in simply seeing—The hero has striven in vain for any preeminency when the student oversees him. The woman who sits in the house and *sees* is a match for a stirring captain. Those still piercing eyes as faithfully exercised on their talent will keep her even with Alexander or Shakespeare. They may go to Asia with parade — or to fairy land, but not beyond her ray. We are as much as we see — Faith is sight and knowledge.

10 April 1841, *Journal* 1: 299–300

My eye is educated to discover anything on the ground, as chestnuts, etc. It is probably wholesomer to look at the ground much than at the heavens.

24 October 1857, *Journal* X: 125

Heaven is under our feet as well as over our heads.

"The Pond in Winter," *Walden*, 283

Many college text-books, which were a weariness and a stumbling-block when *studied*, I have since read a little in with pleasure and profit.

19 February 1854, *Journal* VI: 130

A man receives only what he is ready to receive, whether physically or intellectually or morally, as animals conceive at certain seasons their kind only. We hear and apprehend only what we already half know. If there is something which does not concern me, which is out of my line, which by experience or by genius my attention is not drawn to, however novel and remarkable it may be, if it is spoken we hear it not, if it is written, we read it not, or if we read it, it does not detain us. Every man thus *tracks himself* through life, in all his hearing and reading and observation and travelling. His observations make a chain. The phenomenon or fact that cannot in any wise be linked with the rest which he has observed, he does not observe. By and by we may be ready to receive what we cannot receive now. I find, for example, in Aristotle something about the spawning, etc., of the pout and perch, because I know something about it already and have my attention aroused; but I do not discover till very late that he has made other equally important observations on the spawning of other fishes, because I am not interested in those fishes.

5 January 1860, *Journal* XIII: 77–78

How vain it is to teach youth, or anybody, truths! They can only learn them after their own fashion, and when they get ready. I do not mean by this to condemn our system of education, but to show what it amounts to. A hundred boys at college are drilled in physics and metaphysics, languages, etc. There *may* be one or two in each hundred, prematurely old perchance, who approaches the subject from a similar point of view to his teachers, but as for the rest, and the most promising, it is like agricultural chemistry to so many Indians. They get a valuable drilling, it *may* be, but they do not learn what you profess to teach. They at most only learn where the arsenal is, in case they should ever want to use any of its weapons. The young men, being young, necessarily listen to the lecturer in history, just as they do to the singing of a bird. They expect to be affected by something he may say. It is a kind of poetic pabulum and imagery that they get. Nothing comes quite amiss to their mill.

31 December 1859, *Journal* XIII: 67–68

What does education often do!—It makes a straight-cut ditch of a free, meandering brook.

After 31 October 1850, *Journal* 3: 130

Dr. Bartlett handed me a paper to-day, desiring me to subscribe for a statue to Horace Mann. I declined, and said that I thought a man ought not any more to take up room in the world after he was dead. We shall lose one advantage of a man's dying if we are to have a statue of him forthwith. This is probably meant to be an opposition statue to that of Webster. At this rate they will crowd the streets with them. A man will have to add a clause to his will, "No statue is to be made of me." It is very offensive to my imagination to see the dying stiffen into statues at this rate. We should wait till their bones begin to crumble—and then avoid too near a likeness to the living.

18 September 1859, *Journal* XII: 335

When Allen was here the other day, I found that I could not take two steps with him. He taught school in Concord seventeen years ago, and has not been here since. He wished much to see the town again, but nothing living and fair in it. He had, I should say, a very musty recollection of it. He called on no living creature among all his pupils, but insisted on going to the new buryingground and reading all the epitaphs. I waited at the gate, telling him that the ground did not smell good. I remembered when the first body was placed in it. He did, however, ask after one or two juvenile scamps and one idiotic boy who came to school to him,—how they had turned out,—and also after a certain caged fool, dead since he was here, who had lived near where he boarded; and also after a certain ancient tavern, now pulled down. This at odd intervals, for he improved all the rest of his time while he was here in attending a Sabbath-school convention.

21 October 1855, Journal VII: 505

When I think of the thorough drilling to which young men are subjected in the English universities — acquiring a minute knowledge of Latin prosody & of Greek particles & accents — So that they can not only turn a passage of Homer into English prose or verse — but readily a passage of Shakespeare into Latin hexameters or elegiacs, — that this — and the like of this — is to be liberally education — I am reminded of how different was the education of the actual Homer & Shakespeare — The worthies of the world and liberally educated have always in this sense got along with little Latin & less Greek.

7 August 1852, Journal 5: 287

Scholars have for the most part a diseased way of looking at the world. They mean by it a few cities and importunate assemblies of men and women — who might all be concealed in the grass of the prairie.

They describe their world as old or new — healthy or diseased — according to the state of their libraries — a little dust more or less on their shelves. When I go abroad from under this shingle or slate roof — I find several things which they have not considered — Their conclusions seem imperfect.

1842–44, Journal 2: 69

I have met with some barren accomplished gentlemen who seemed to have been to school all their lives and never had a vacation to live in. Oh, if they could only have been stolen by the Gypsies! They had better have died in infancy and been buried under the leaves, their lips besmeared with blackberries, and Cock Robin for their sexton.

20 October 1855, *Journal* VII: 503

What avail all your scholarly accomplishments and learning, compared with wisdom and manhood? To omit his other behavior, see what a work this comparatively unread and unlettered man wrote within six weeks. Where is our professor of *belles lettres* or of logic and rhetoric, who can write so well? He wrote in prison, not a history of the world, like Raleigh, but an American book which I think will live longer than that. I do not know of such words, uttered under such circumstances, and so copiously withal, in Roman or English or any history.

"The Last Days of John Brown,"
Reform Papers, 150

He did not go to the college called Harvard, good old Alma Mater as she is. He was not fed on the pap that is there furnished. As he phrased it, "I know no more of grammar than one of your calves." But he went to the great university of the West, where he sedulously pursued the study of Liberty, for which he had early betrayed a fondness, and having taken many degrees, he finally commenced the public practice of Humanity in Kansas, as you all know. Such were *his humanities,* and not any study of grammar. He would have left a Greek accent slanting the wrong way, and righted up a falling man.

"A Plea for Captain John Brown,"
Reform Papers, 113

If Paris is much in your mind, if it is more and more to you, Concord is less and less, and yet it would be a wretched bargain to accept the proudest Paris in exchange for my native village. At best, Paris could only be a school in which to learn to live here, a stepping-stone to Concord, a school in which to fit for this university. I wish so to live ever as to derive my satisfactions and inspirations from the commonest events, every-day phenomena, so that what my senses hourly perceive, my daily walk, the conversation of my neighbors, may inspire me, and I may dream of no heaven but that which lies about me. A man may acquire a taste for wine or brandy, and so lose his love for water, but should we not pity him?

The sight of a marsh hawk in Concord meadows is worth more to me than the entry of the allies into Paris. In this sense I am not ambitious. I do not wish my native soil to become exhausted and run out through neglect. Only that travelling is good which reveals to me the value of home and enables me to enjoy it better.

10 March 1856, Journal VIII: 204–5

The value of these wild fruits is not in the mere possession or eating of them, but in the sight or enjoyment of them. The very derivation of the word "fruit" would suggest this. It is from the Latin *fructus*, meaning that which is *used* or *enjoyed*. If it were not so, then going a-berrying and going to market would be nearly synonymous expressions. Of course it is the spirit in which you do a thing which makes it interesting, whether it is sweeping a room or pulling turnips. Peaches are unquestionably a very beautiful and palatable fruit, but the gathering of them for the market is not nearly so interesting as the gathering of huckleberries for your own use.

A man fits out a ship at a great expense and sends it to the West Indies with a crew of men and boys, and after six months or a year it comes back with a load of pineapples. Now, if no more gets accomplished than the speculator commonly aims at, — if it simply turns out what is called a successful venture, — I am less interested in this expedition than in some child's first excursion a-huckleberrying, in which it is introduced into a new world, experiences a new development, though it brings home only a gill of huckleberries in its basket. I know that the newspapers and politicians declare otherwise, but they do not alter the fact. Then, I think that the fruit of the latter expedition was finer than that of the former. It was a more fruitful expedition. The value of any experience is measured, of course, not by the amount of money, but the amount of development we get out of it. If a New England boy's dealings with oranges and pineapples have had more to do with his development than picking huckleberries or pulling turnips have, then he rightly and naturally thinks more of the former; otherwise not.

Do not think that the fruits of New England are mean and insignificant, while those of some foreign land are noble and memorable. Our own, whatever they may be, are far more important to us than any others can be. They educate us, and fit us to live in New England. Better for us is the wild strawberry than the pineapple, the wild apple than the orange, the hazelnut or pignut than the cocoanut or almond, and not on account of their flavor merely, but the part they play in our education.

26 November 1860, *Journal* XIV: 273–74

How many schools I have thought of which I might go to but did not go to! expecting foolishly that some greater advantages or schooling would come to me! It is these comparatively cheap and private expeditions that substantiate our existence and batten our lives, as, where a vine touches the earth in its undulating course, it puts forth roots and thickens its stock. Our employment generally is tinkering, mending the old worn-out teapot of society. Our stock in trade is solder. Better for me, says my genius, to go cranberrying this afternoon for the *Vaccinium Oxycoccus* in Gowing's Swamp, to get but a pocketful and learn its peculiar flavor, aye, and the flavor of Gowing's Swamp and of *life* in New England, than to go consul to Liverpool and get I don't know how many thousand dollars for it, with no such flavor. Many of our days should be spent, not in vain expectations and lying on our oars, but in carrying out deliberately and faithfully the hundred little purposes which every man's genius must have suggested to him. Let not your life be wholly without an object, though it be only the quality of an insignificant berry that you will have tasted, but the flavor of your life to that extent, and it will be such sauce as no wealth can buy.

Both a conscious and an unconscious life are good. Neither is good exclusively, for both have the same source. The wisely conscious life springs out of an unconscious suggestion. I have found my account in travelling in having prepared beforehand a list of questions which I would get answered, not trusting to my interest at the moment, and can then travel with the most profit. Indeed, it is by obeying the suggestions of a higher light within you that you escape from yourself and, in the transit, as it were see with the unworn sides of your eye, travel totally new paths. What is that pretend life that does not take up a claim, that does not occupy ground, that cannot build a causeway to its objects, that sits on a bank looking over a bog, singing its desires?

30 August 1856, *Journal* IX: 36–38

Each town should have a park, or rather a primitive forest, of five hundred or a thousand acres, where a stick should never be cut for fuel, a common possession forever, for instruction and recreation. We hear of cow-commons and ministerial lots, but we want *men*-commons and lay lots, inalienable forever. Let us keep the New World *new*, preserve all the advantages of living in the country. There is meadow and pasture and wood-lot for the town's poor. Why not a forest and huckleberry-field for the town's rich? All Walden Wood might have been preserved for our park forever, with Walden in its midst, and the Easterbrooks Country, an unoccupied area of some four square miles, might have been our huckleberry-field. If any owners of these tracts are about to leave the world without natural heirs who need or deserve to be specially remembered, they will do wisely to abandon their possession to all, and not will them to some individual who perhaps has enough already. As some give to Harvard College or another institution, why might not another give a forest or huckleberry field to Concord? A town is an institution which deserves to be remembered. We boast of our system of education, but why stop at schoolmasters and schoolhouses? We are all schoolmasters, and our schoolhouse is the universe. To attend chiefly to the desk or schoolhouse while we neglect the scenery in which it is placed is absurd. If we do not look out we shall find our fine schoolhouse standing in a cow-yard at last.

A river, with its waterfalls and meadows, a lake, a hill, a cliff or individual rocks, a forest and ancient trees standing singly. Such things are beautiful; they have a high use which dollars and cents never represent. If the inhabitants of a town were wise, they would seek to preserve these things, though at a considerable expense; for such things educate far more than any hired teachers or preachers, or any at present recognized system of school education.

These bright leaves are not the exception but the rule, for I believe that *all* leaves, even grasses, etc., etc.,—*Panicum clandestinum,*—and mosses, as sphagnum, under favorable circumstances acquire brighter colors just before their fall. When you come to observe faithfully the changes of each humblest plant, you find it may be unexpectedly, that each has sooner or later its peculiar autumnal tint or tints, though it may be rare and unobserved, as many a plant is at all seasons. And if you undertake to make a complete list of the bright tints, your list will be as long as a catalogue of the plants in your vicinity.

Think how much the eyes of painters, both artisans and artists, and of the manufacturers of cloth and paper, and the paper-stainers, etc., are to be educated by these autumnal colors. The stationer's envelopes may be of very various tints, yet not so various as those of the leaves of a single tree sometimes. If you want a different shade or tint of a particular color, you have only to look further within or without the tree, or the wood. The eye might thus be taught to distinguish color and appreciate a difference of tint or shade.

22 October 1858, Journal XI: 240

The observatory was a building of considerable size, erected by the students of Williamstown College, whose buildings might be seen by daylight gleaming far down in the valley. It would be no small advantage if every college were thus located at the base of a mountain, as good at least as one well-endowed professorship. It were as well to be educated in the shadow of a mountain as in more classical shades. Some will remember, no doubt, not only that they went to the college, but that they went to the mountain. Every visit to its summit would, as it were, generalize the particular information gained below, and subject it to more catholic tests.

"Tuesday," A Week on the Concord
and Merrimack Rivers, 187

I went to the woods because I wished to live deliberately, to front only the essential facts of life, and see if I could not learn what it had to teach, and not, when I came to die, discover that I had not lived. I did not wish to live what was not life, living is so dear; nor did I wish to practise resignation, unless it was quite necessary. I wanted to live deep and suck out all the marrow of life, to live so sturdily and Spartan-like as to put to rout all that was not life, to cut a broad swath and shave close, to drive life into a corner, reduce it to its lowest terms, and, if it proved to

be mean, why then to get the whole and genuine meanness of it, and publish its meanness to the world; or if it
were sublime, to know it by experience, and be able to
give a true account of it in my next excursion.

> "Where I Lived, and What I
> Lived For," *Walden*, 90–91

If you stand right fronting and face to face to a fact, you
will see the sun glimmer on both its surfaces, as if it were
a cimeter [scimitar], and feel its sweet edge dividing you
through the heart and marrow, and so you will happily
conclude your mortal career. Be it life or death, we crave
only reality. If we are really dying, let us hear the rattle in
our throats and feel cold in the extremities; if we are alive,
let us go about our business.

> "Where I Lived, and What I
> Lived For," *Walden*, 98

The frontiers are not east or west, north or south, but
wherever a man *fronts* a fact, though that fact be his
neighbor, there is an unsettled wilderness between him
and Canada, between him and the setting sun, or further
still, between him and it. Let him build himself a log-
house with the bark on where he is, *fronting* IT, and wage
there an Old French war for seven years or seventy years,
with Indians and Rangers, or whatever else may come
between him and the reality, and save his scalp if he can.

> "Thursday," *A Week on the Concord
> and Merrimack Rivers*, 304

How novel and original must be each new mans view of
the universe — for though the world is so old — & so
many books have been written — each object appears

wholly undescribed to our experience—each field of thought wholly unexplored—The whole world is an America—a *New World.*

It is worth the while to apply what wisdom one has to the conduct of his life surely. I find my self oftenest wise in little things & foolish in great ones. That I may accomplish some particular petty affair well I live my whole life coarsely. A broad margin of leisure is as beautiful in a man's life as in a book. Haste makes waste no less in life than in housekeeping. Keep the time—observe the hours of the universe—not of the cars. What are 3 score years & ten hurriedly & coarsely lived to moments of divine leisure, in which your life is coincident with the life of the Universe. We live too fast & coarsely just as we eat too fast & do not know the true savor of our food. We consult our will & understanding and the expectation of men—not our genius. I can impose upon myself tasks which will crush me for life and prevent all expansion—& this I am but too inclined to do. One moment of life costs many hours,—hours not of business but of preparation and invitation. Yet the man who does not betake himself at once & desperately to sawing wood is called a loafer—though he may be knocking at the doors of heaven—all the while which shall surely be opened to him—That aim in life is highest which requires the highest & finest discipline. How much—What infinite leisure it requires—as of a lifetime, to appreciate a single phenomenon! You must camp down beside it as for life—having reached your land of promise & give yourself wholly to it.

Men esteem truth remote, in the outskirts of the system, behind the farthest star, before Adam and after the last man. In eternity there is indeed something true and sublime. But all these times and places and occasions are now and here. God himself culminates in the present moment, and will never be more divine in the lapse of all the ages. And we are enabled to apprehend at all what is sublime and noble only by the perpetual instilling and drenching of the reality which surrounds us. The universe constantly and obediently answers to our conceptions; whether we travel fast or slow, the track is laid for us. Let us spend our lives in conceiving then. The poet or artist never had so fair and noble a design but some of his posterity at least could accomplish it.

"Where I Lived, and What I
Lived For," *Walden*, 96–97

It is essential that a man confine himself to pursuits — a scholar, for instance, to studies — which lie next to and conduce to his life, which do not go against the grain, either of his will or his imagination. The scholar finds in his experience some studies to be most fertile and radiant with light, others dry, barren, and dark. If he is wise, he will not persevere in the last, as a plant in a cellar will strive toward the light. He will confine the observations of his mind as closely as possible to the experience or life of his senses. His thought must live with and be inspired with the life of the body. The deathbed scenes and observations even of the best and wisest afford but a sorry picture of our humanity. Some men endeavor to live a constrained life, to subject their whole lives to their wills, as he who said he would give a sign if he were conscious after his head was cut off, — but he gave no sign. Dwell as near as possible to the channel in which your life flows. A man may associate with such companions, he may pursue such employments, as will darken the day for him. Men choose darkness rather than light.

10 March 1853, *Journal* V: 16–17

A man thinks as well through his legs and arms as his brain. We exaggerate the importance and exclusiveness of the headquarters. Do you suppose they were a race of consumptives and dyspeptics who invented Grecian mythology and poetry? The poet's words are, "You would almost say the body thought!" I quite say it. I trust we have a good body then.

31 December 1859, *Journal* XIII: 69–70

We reason from our hands to our head.

5 September 1851, *Journal* 4: 46

It is true enough, Cambridge college is really beginning to wake up and redeem its character and overtake the age. I see by the catalogue that they are about establishing a scientific school in connection with the university, at which any one above eighteen, on paying one hundred dollars annually, may be instructed in the highest branches of science, — in astronomy, "theoretical and practical, with the use of the instruments" (so the great Yankee astronomer may be born without delay), in mechanics and engineering in the last degree.... They have been foolish enough to put at the end of all this earnest the old joke of a diploma. Let every sheep keep but his own skin, I say.

Letter to Emerson, 14 November 1847,
Correspondence, 190

The State commonly grants a tract of forest to make an academy out of, for such is the material of which our institutions are made, though only the crudest part of it is used, but the groves of the academy are straightway cut down, and that institution is built of its lumber, its coarsest and least valuable part. Down go the groves of the academy and up goes its frame, — on some bare common far away.

8 March 1858, *Journal* X: 297

We saw one schoolhouse on our walk and listened to the sounds which issued from it; but it appeared like a place where the process, not of enlightening, but of obfuscating the mind was going on, and the pupils received only so much light as could penetrate the shadow of the Catholic church.

"A Yankee in Canada," *Excursions*, 46

In society — in the best institutions of men — I remark a certain precocity — When we should be growing children — we are already little men. Infants as we are we make haste to be weaned from our great mother's breast & cultivate our parts by intercourse with one another.

I have not much faith in the method of restoring impoverished soils which relies on manuring mainly — & does not add some virgin soil or muck

Many a poor sore eyed student that I have heard of would grow faster both intellectually & physically if instead of sitting up so very late to study, he honestly slumbered a fool's allowance.

13 February 1851, *Journal* 3: 191–92

A nation may be ever so civilized and yet lack wisdom. Wisdom is the result of education, and education being the bringing out, or development, of that which is in a man, by contact with the Not Me, is safer in the hands of Nature than of Art. The savage may be, and often is, a sage. Our Indian is more of a man than the inhabitant of a city. He lives as a man—he thinks as a man—he dies as a man. The latter, it is true, is more learned; Learning is Art's creature; but it is not essential to the perfect man —it cannot educate. A man may spend his days in the study of a single species of animalculae, invisible to the naked eye, and thus become the founder of a new branch of science, without having advanced the great object for which life was given him at all.

The naturalist, the chemist, or the mechanist, is no more a man for all his learning. Life is still as short as ever, death as inevitable, and the heavens are as far off.

Early Essays and Miscellanies, 110–11

Not by constraint or severity shall you have access to true wisdom, but by abandonment and childlike mirthfulness. If you would know aught, be gay before it.

23 June 1840, *Journal* 1: 140

Age is no better, hardly so well, qualified for an instructor as youth, for it has not profited so much as it has lost. One may almost doubt if the wisest man has learned any thing of absolute value by living. Practically, the old have no very important advice to give the young, their own experience has been so partial, and their lives have been such miserable failures, for private reasons, as they must believe; and it may be that they have some faith left which belies that experience, and they are only less young than they were. I have lived some thirty years on this planet, and I have yet to hear the first syllable of valuable or even earnest advice from my seniors. They have told me nothing, and probably cannot tell me any thing, to the purpose. Here is life, an experiment to a great extent untried by me; but it does not avail me that they have tried it. If I have any experience which I think valuable, I am sure to reflect that this my Mentors said nothing about.

"Economy," *Walden*, 8–9

Most people with whom I talk, men and women even of some originality and genius, have their scheme of the universe all cut and dried,—very *dry*, I assure you, to hear, dry enough to burn, dry-rotted and powder-post, methinks,—which they set up between you and them in the shortest intercourse; an ancient and tottering frame with all its boards blown off. They do not walk without their bed. Some to me seemingly very unimportant and unsubstantial things and relations are for them everlastingly settled,—as Father, Son, and Holy Ghost, and the like. These are like the everlasting hills to them. But in all my wanderings, I never came across the least vestige of authority for these things. They have not left so distinct a trace as the delicate flower of a remote geological period on the coal in my grate. The wisest man preaches no doctrines; he has no scheme; he sees no rafter, not even a cobweb, against the heavens. It is clear sky.

"Sunday," *A Week on the Concord and Merrimack River*, 69–70

The senses of children are unprofaned   their whole body is one sense—they take a physical pleasure in rid-

ing on a rail—they love to teter—so does the unviolated
—the unsophisticated mind derive an inexpressible pleasure from the simplest exercise of thoughts.

7 July 1851, *Journal* 3: 291

Children, who play life, discern its true law and relations
more clearly than men, who fail to live it worthily, but
who think that they are wiser by experience, that is, by
failure.

"Where I Lived, and What
I Lived For," *Walden*, 96

It appears to me that at a very early age—the mind of
man—perhaps at the same time with his body, ceases to
be elastic. His intellectual power becomes something defined—& limited. He does not think as expansively as he
would stretch himself in his growing days—What was
flexible sap hardens into heartwood and there is no further change. In the season of youth methinks man is ca-
pable of intellectual effort & performance which sur-
passes all rules & bounds—As the youth lays out his
whole strength without fear or prudence & does not feel
his limits. It is the transition from poetry to prose. The
young man can run & leap—he has not learned exactly
how far—he knows no limits—The grown man does not
exceed his daily labor. He has no strength to waste.

17 January 1852, *Journal* 4: 265–66

The last new journal thinks that it is very liberal, nay
bold, but dares not publish a child's thought on important subjects such as life and death and good books. It requires sanction of the divines just as surely as the tamest
journal does. If it had been published at the time of the

famous dispute between Christ and the doctors, it would have published only the opinions of the doctors and suppressed Christ's.

Remember thy creator in the days of thy youth. i.e. Lay up a store of natural influences — sing while you may before the evil days come — he that hath ears let him hear — see — hear smell — taste — & c while these senses are fresh & pure

There is always a kind of fine Aeolian harp music to be heard in the air — I hear now as it were the mellow sound of distant horns in the hollow mansions of the upper air — a sound to make all men divinely insane that hear it — far away over head subsiding into my ear. to ears that are expanded what a harp this world is!

How few valuable observations can we make in youth — What if there were united the susceptibility of youth with the discrimination of age.

I served my apprenticeship and have since done considerable journey-work in the huckleberry-field, though I never paid for my schooling and clothing in that way. It was itself some of the best schooling I got, and paid for itself.

I have spent many an hour, when I was younger, floating over its surface as the zephyr willed, having paddled my boat to the middle, and lying on my back across the seats, in a summer forenoon, dreaming awake, until I was roused by the boat touching the sand, and I arose to see what shore my fates had impelled me to; days when idleness was the most attractive and productive industry. Many a forenoon have I stolen away, preferring to spend thus the most valued part of the day; for I was rich, if not in money, in sunny hours and summer days, and spent them lavishly; nor do I regret that I did not waste more of them in the workshop or the teacher's desk.

"The Ponds," *Walden*, 191–92

Men say they know many things;
But lo! They have taken wings, —
The arts and sciences,
And a thousand appliances;
The wind that blows
Is all that any body knows.

"Economy," *Walden*, 42

How few ever get beyond feeding, clothing, sheltering, and warming themselves in this world, and begin to treat themselves as human beings, — as intellectual and moral beings! Most seem not to see any further, — not to see over the ridge-pole of their barns, — or to be exhausted and accomplish nothing more than a full barn, though it may be accompanied by an empty head. They venture a little, run some risks, when it is a question of a larger crop of corn or potatoes; but they are commonly timid and count their coppers, when the question is whether their children shall be educated. He who has the reputation of being the thriftiest farmer and making the best bargains is really the most thriftless and makes the worst. It is safest to invest in knowledge, for the probability is that you can carry that with you wherever you go.

3 January 1861, *Journal* XIV: 306

There is a still life in America that is little observed or dreamed of. Here were possible auditors and critics which the lecturer at the Lyceum last night did not think of. How smug they are somewhere under the snow now, not to be thought of, if it were not for these pretty tracks! And for a week, or fortnight even, of pretty still weather the tracks will remain, to tell of the nocturnal adventures of a tiny mouse who was not beneath the notice of the Lord. So it was so many thousands of years before Gutenberg invented printing with *his* types, and so it will be so many thousands of years after his types are forgotten perchance. The deer mouse will be printing on the snow of Well Meadow to be read by a new race of men.

15 January 1857, *Journal* IX: 223–24

I think that most men, as farmers, hunters, fishers, etc., walk along a river's bank, or paddle along its stream, without seeing the reflections. Their minds are not abstracted from the surface, from surfaces generally. It is only a reflecting mind that sees reflections. I am often aware that I have been occupied with shallow and commonplace thoughts, looking for something superficial, when I did not see the most glorious reflections, though exactly in the line of my vision. If the fisherman was looking at the reflection, he would not know when he had a nibble! I know from my own experience that he may cast his line right over the most elysian landscape and sky, and not *catch* the slightest notion of them. You must be in an abstract mood to see reflections, however distinct. I was even startled by the sight of that reflected red oak as if it were a water-spirit. When we are enough abstracted, the opaque earth itself reflects images to us; i.e., we are imaginative, see visions, etc. Such a reflection, this inky, leafy tree against the white sky, can only be seen at this season.

2 November 1857, *Journal* X: 156–57

There is no such thing as purely *objective* observation. Your observation, to be interesting, i.e. to be significant, must be *subjective*. The sum of what the writer of whatever class has to report is simply some human experience, whether he be poet or philosopher or man of science. The man of most science is the man most alive, whose life is the greatest event. Senses that take cognizance of outward things merely are of no avail. It matters not where or how far you travel, — the farther commonly the worse, — but how much alive you are. If it is possible to conceive of an event outside to humanity, it is not of the slightest significance, though it were the explosion of a planet. Every important worker will report what life there is in him. It makes no odds into what seeming deserts the poet is born. Though all his neighbors pronounce it a Sahara, it will be a paradise to him; for the desert which we see is the result of the barrenness of our experience. No mere willful activity whatever, whether in writing verses or collecting statistics, will produce true poetry or science. If you are really a sick man, it is indeed to be regretted, for you cannot accomplish so much as if you were well. All that a man has to say or do that can possibly concern mankind, is in some shape or other to tell the story of his love, — to sing; and, if he is fortunate and keeps alive, he will be forever in love. This alone is to be alive to the extremities. It is a pity that this divine creature should ever suffer from cold feet; a still greater pity that the coldness so often reaches his heart. I look over the report of the doings of a scientific association and am surprised that there is so little life to be reported; I am put off with a parcel of dry technical terms. Anything living is easily and naturally expressed in popular language. I cannot help suspecting that the life of these learned professors has been almost as inhuman and wooden as a rain-gauge or self-registering magnetic machine. They communicate no fact which rises to the temperature of blood-heat. It doesn't all amount to one rhyme.

6 May 1854, *Journal* VI: 236–38

Let us not underrate the value of a fact; it will one day flower into a truth. It is astonishing how few facts of importance are added in a century to the natural history of any animal. The natural history of man himself is still being gradually written. Men are knowing enough after their fashion. Every countryman and dairy-maid knows that the coats of the fourth stomach of the calf will curdle milk, and what particular mushroom is a safe and nutritious diet. You cannot go into any field or wood, but it will seem as if every stone had been turned, and the bark on every tree ripped up. But, after all, it is much easier to discover than to see when the cover is off. It has been well said that "the attitude of inspection is prone." Wisdom does not inspect, but behold. We must look a long time before we can see. Slow are the beginnings of philosophy. He has something demoniacal in him, who can discern a law or couple two facts. We can imagine a time when "Water runs down hill" may have been taught in the schools. The true man of science will know nature better by his finer organization; he will smell, taste, see, hear, feel, better than other men. His will be a deeper and finer experience. We do not learn by inference and deduction and the application of mathematics to philosophy, but by direct intercourse and sympathy. It is with science and with ethics, — we cannot know the truth by contrivance and method; the Baconian is as false as any other, and with all the helps of machinery and the arts, the most scientific will still be the healthiest and friendliest man, and possess a more perfect Indian wisdom.

"Natural History of Massachusetts,"
The Natural History Essays, 28–29

I think that the man of science makes this mistake, and the mass of mankind along with him: that you should coolly give your chief attention to the phenomenon which excites you as something independent of you, and not as it is related to you. The important fact is its effect on me. He thinks that I have no business to see anything else but just what he defines the rainbow to be, but I care not whether my vision of truth is a waking thought or a dream remembered, whether it is seen in the light or in the dark. It is the subject of the vision, the truth alone, that concerns me. The philosopher for whom rainbows, etc., can be explained away never saw them. With regard to such objects I find that it is not that they themselves (with which the men of science deal) that concern me;

the point of interest is somewhere *between* me and them (i.e. the objects).

We have heard much about the poetry of mathematics, but very little of it has yet been sung. The ancients had a juster notion of their poetic value than we. The most distinct and beautiful statement of any truth must take at last the mathematical form. We might so simplify the rules of moral philosophy, as well of arithmetic, that one formula would express them both. All the moral laws are readily translated into natural philosophy, for often we have only to restore the primitive meaning of the words by which they are expressed, or to attend to their literal instead of their metaphorical sense. They are already *supernatural* philosophy. The whole body of what is now called moral or ethical truth existed in the golden age as abstract science. Or, if we prefer, we may say that the laws of Nature are the purest morality. The Tree of Knowledge is a Tree of Knowledge of good and evil. He is not a true man of science who does not bring more sympathy to his studies, and expect to learn something by behavior as well as by application. It is childish to rest in the discovery of mere coincidences, or of partial and extraneous laws. The study of geometry is a petty and idle exercise of the mind, if it is applied to no larger system than the starry one. Mathematics should be mixed not only with physics but the ethics, *that* is *mixed* mathematics. The fact which interests us most is the life of the naturalist. The purest science is still biographical. Nothing will dignify and elevate science while it is sundered so wholly from the moral life of its devotee, and he professes another religion than it teaches, and worships at a foreign shrine. Anciently the faith of a philosopher was identical with his system, or in other words, his view of the universe. My friends mistake when they communicate facts to me with so much pains. Their presence, even their exaggerations and loose statements, are equally good facts for me. I have no respect for facts even except when I would use them, and for the most part I am independent of those which I hear, and can afford to be inaccurate, or, in other words, to substitute more present and pressing facts in their place.

"Friday," *A Week on the Concord
and Merrimack Rivers*, 362–63

I have a common place book for facts and another for poetry — but I find it difficult always to preserve the vague distinction which I had in my mind — for the most interesting & beautiful facts are so much the more poetry and that is their success. They are *translated* from earth to heaven — I see that if my facts were sufficiently vital & significant — perhaps transmuted more into the substance of the human mind — I should need but one book of poetry to contain them all.

18 February 1852, *Journal* 4: 356

We should read history as little critically as we consider the landscape, and be more interested by the atmospheric tints and various lights and shades which the intervening spaces create than by its groundwork and composition. It is the morning now turned evening and seen in the west, — the same sun, but a new light and atmosphere. Its beauty is like the sunset; not a fresco painting on a wall, flat and bounded, but atmospheric and roving or free. In reality, history fluctuates as the face of the landscape from morning to evening. What is of moment is its hue and color. Time hides no treasures; we want not its *then* but its *now*. We do not complain that the mountains in the horizon are blue and indistinct; they are the more like the heavens.

Of what moment are facts that can be lost,—which need to be commemorated? The monument of death will outlast the memory of the dead. The Pyramids do not tell the tale which was confided to them; the living fact commemorates itself. Why look in the dark for light? Strictly speaking, the historical societies have not recovered one fact from oblivion, but are themselves instead of the fact that is lost. The researcher is more memorable than the researched. The crowd stood admiring the mist and the dim outlines of the trees seen though it, when one of their number advanced to explore the phenomenon, and with fresh admiration all eyes turned on his dimly retreating figure. It is astonishing with how little cooperation of the societies the past is remembered. Its story indeed had another muse than has been assigned it. There is a good instance of the manner in which all history began, in Alkwakidis' Arabian Chronicle: "I was informed by *Almed Almatin Aljorhami*, who had it from *Rephaa Ebn Kais Alamiri*, who had it from *Saiph Ebn Fabalah Alchatquarmi*, who had it from *Thabet Ebn Alkamah*, who said he was present at the action." These fathers of history were not anxious to preserve, but to learn the fact; uncover the past; the *past* cannot be *presented*; we cannot know what we are not. But one veil hangs over past, present, and future, and it is the province of the historian to find out, not what was, but what is. Where a battle has been fought, you will find nothing but the bones of men and beasts; where a battle is being fought, there are hearts beating. We will sit on a mound and muse, and not try to make these skeletons stand on their legs again. Does Nature remember, think you, that they *were* men, or not rather that they *are* bones?

"Monday," *A Week on the Concord and Merrimack Rivers,* 154–55

Most of the stone a nation hammers goes toward its tomb only. It buries itself alive. As for the Pyramids, there is nothing to wonder at in them so much as the fact that so many men could be found degraded enough to spend their lives constructing a tomb for some ambitious booby, whom it would have been wiser and manlier to have drowned in the Nile, and then given his body to the dogs.

"Economy," *Walden,* 58

It would seem as if the very language of our parlors would lose all its nerve and degenerate into *palaver* wholly, our lives pass at such remoteness from its symbols, and its metaphors and tropes are necessarily so far fetched, through slides and dumb-waiters, as it were; in other words, the parlor is so far from the kitchen and workshop. The dinner even is only the parable of a dinner, commonly. As if only the savage dwelt near enough to Nature and Truth to borrow a trope from them. How can the scholar, who dwells away in the North West Territory or the Isle of Man, tell what is parliamentary in the kitchen?

"House-Warming," *Walden,* 244–45

Meanwhile my beans, the length of whose rows added together, was seven miles already planted, were impatient to be hoed, for the earliest had grown considerably before the latest were in the ground; indeed they were not easily to be put off. What was the meaning of this so steady and self-respecting, this small Herculean labor, I knew not. I came to love my rows, my beans, though so many more than I wanted. They attached me to the earth, and so I got strength like Antaeus.

"The Bean-Field," *Walden*, 155

Write often write upon a thousand themes—rather than long at a time—Not trying to turn too many feeble summersets in the air—& so come down upon your head at least—Antaeus like be not long absent from the ground —Those sentences are good and well discharged which are like so many little resiliencies from the spring floor of our life.—a distinct fruit & kernel itself—springing from terra-firma.

12 December 1851, *Journal* 4: 177–78

Not that I wanted beans to eat, for I am by nature a Pythagorean, so far as beans are concerned, whether they mean porridge or voting, and exchanged them for rice; but, perchance, as some must work in fields if only for the sake of tropes and expression, to serve a parable-maker one day.

"The Bean-Field," *Walden*, 162

Where is the literature which gives expression to Nature? He would be a poet who could impress the winds and streams into his service, to speak for him; who nailed words to their primitive senses, as farmers drive down stakes in the spring, which the frost has heaved; who derived his words as often as he used them,—transplanted them to his page with earth adhering to their roots; whose words were so true and fresh and natural that they would appear to expand like the buds at the approach of spring, though they lay half smothered between two musty leaves in a library,—aye, to bloom and bear fruit there, after their kind, annually, for the faithful reader, in sympathy with surrounding Nature.

"Walking," *The Natural History Essays*, 120

He is richest who has most use for nature as raw material of tropes and symbols with which to describe his life. If these gates of golden willow affect me, they correspond to the beauty and promise of some experience on which I am entering. If I am overflowing with life, and rich in experience for which I lack expression, then nature will be my language full of poetry,—all nature will *fable*, and every natural phenomenon be a myth. The man of science, who is not seeking for expression but for a fact to be expressed merely, studies nature as a dead language. I pray for such inward experience as will make nature significant.

10 May 1853, *Journal* V: 135

As in the expression of moral truths we admire any closeness to the physical fact which in all language is the symbol of the spiritual, so, finally, when natural objects are described, it is an advantage if words derived originally from nature, it is true, but which have been turned (*tropes*) from their primary signification to a moral sense are used, i.e., if the object is personified. The one who loves and understands a thing the best will incline to use the personal pronoun in speaking of it.

16 February 1860, *Journal* XII: 147–48

Is it not as language that all natural objects affect the poet? He sees a flower or other object, and it is beautiful or affecting to him because it is a symbol of his thought, and what he indistinctly feels or perceives is matured in some other organization. The objects I behold correspond to my mood.

7 August 1853, *Journal* V: 359

Shall I not have words as fresh as my thought—? Shall I use any other man's word? A genuine thought or feeling can find expression for itself, if it have to invent hieroglyphics. It has the universe for type metal. It is for want of original thought that one man's style is like another's.

8 September 1851, *Journal* 3: 61

How hard one must work in order to acquire his language,—words by which to express himself! I have known a particular rush, for instance, for at least twenty years, but I have ever been prevented from describing some [of] its peculiarities, because I did not know its name nor any one in the neighborhood who could tell me it. With the knowledge of the name comes a distincter recognition and knowledge of the thing. That shore is now more describable, and poetic even. My knowledge was cramped and confined before, and grew rusty because not used,—for it could not be used. My knowledge now becomes communicable and grows by communication. I can now learn what others know about the same thing.

Talk about learning our *letters* and being *literate!* Why, the roots of *letters* are *things*. Natural objects and phenomena are the original symbols or types which express our thought and feelings, and yet American scholars, having little or no root in the soil, commonly strive with all their might to confine themselves to the imported symbols alone. All the true growth and experience, the living speech, they would fain reject as "Americanisms." It is the old error, which the church, the state, the school ever commit, choosing darkness rather than light, holding fast to the old and to tradition. A more intimate knowledge, a deeper experience, will surely originate a word. When I really know that our river pursues a serpentine course to the Merrimack, shall I continue to describe it by referring to some other river no older than itself which is like it, and call it a *meander*? It is no more *meandering* than the Meander is *musketaquidding*. As well sing of the nightingale here as the Meander. What if there were a tariff on words, on language, of the encouragement of home manufactures? Let the schoolmaster distinguish the true from the counterfeit.

As for themes — say first "Miscellaneous Thoughts" — set one up to a window to note what passes in the street, and make her comments thereon; or let her gaze in the fire, or into a corner where there is a spider's web, and philosophize — moralize — theorize, or what not.

What their hands find to putter about, or their minds to think about, — that let them write about. To say nothing of Advantages or disadvantages — of this, that, or the other. Let them set down their ideas at any given Season — preserving the chain of thought as complete as may be.

This is the style pedagogical.

> Letter to Helen Thoreau, 6 October 1838,
> *Correspondence*, 29

The Scripture rule, "Unto him that hath shall be given," is true of composition. The more you have thought and written on a given theme, the more you can still write. Thought breeds thought. It grows under your hands.

> 13 February 1860, *Journal* XIII: 145

When I hear the hypercritical quarreling about grammar and style, the position of the particles, etc., etc., stretching or contracting every speaker to certain rules of theirs, — Mr. Webster, perhaps, not having spoken according to Mr. Kirkham's rule, — I see that they forget the first requisite and rule is that expression shall be vital and natural, as much as the voice of a brute or an interjection: first of all, mother tongue; and last of all, artificial or father tongue. Essentially your truest poetic sentence is as free and lawless as a lamb's bleat. The grammarian is often one who can neither cry nor laugh, yet thinks that he can express human emotions. So the posture-masters tell you how you shall walk, — turning your toes out, perhaps, excessively, — but so the beautiful walkers are not made.

> 2 January 1859, *Journal* XI: 386

When I read some of the rules for speaking and writing the English language correctly, — as that a sentence must never end with a particle, — and perceive how implicitly even the learned obey it, I think —

> Any fool can make a rule
> And every fool will mind it.

2 February 1860, *Journal* XIII: 125

The forcible writer stands bodily behind his words with his experience — He does not make books out of books, but he has been *there* in person.

3 February 1852, *Journal* 4: 326

We have our times of action and our times of reflection — the one mood caters for the other — Now I am Alexander — and then I am Homer. One while my hand is impatient to handle an axe or hoe, and at another to pen. I am sure I write the tougher truth for these calluses on my palms. They give firmness to the sentence.

The sentences of a laboring man are like hardened thongs — or the sinews of the deer — or the roots of the pine.

23 March 1842, *Journal* 1: 388

It would be a truer discipline for the writer to take the least film of thought that floats in the twilight sky of his mind for his theme — about which he has scarcely one idea (that would be teaching his ideas how to shoot) faintest intimations — shadowiest subjects — make a lecture on this — by assiduity and attention get perchance two views of the same — increase a little the stock of knowledge — clear a new field instead of manuring the old — Instead of making a lecture out of such obvious truths — hacknied to the minds of all thinkers — We see too soon to ally the perceptions of the mind to the experience of the hand — to prove our gossamer truths practical — to show their connexion with our every day life (better show their distance from our every day life) to relate them to the cider mill and the banking institution. Ah give me pure mind — pure thought. Let me not be in haste to detect the *universal law*, let me see more clearly a particular instance. Much finer themes I aspire to — which will yield no satisfaction to the vulgar mind — not one sentence for them — Perchance it may convince such that there are more things in heaven & earth than are dreamed of in their philosophy. Dissolve one nebula — & so destroy the nebular system & hypothesis. Do not seek expressions — seek thoughts to be expressed. By perseverance you get two views of the same rare truth.

25 December 1851, *Journal* 4: 222–23

How vain it is to sit down to write when you have not stood up to live! Methinks that the moment my legs begin to move my thoughts begin to flow — as if I had given vent to the stream at the lower end & consequently new fountains flowed into it at the upper. A thousand rills which have their rise in the sources of thought — burst forth & fertilise my brain. you need to increase the draught below — as the owners of meadows on C. river say of Billerica Dam. Only while we are in action is the circulation perfect. The writing which consists with habitual sitting is mechanical wooden dull to read.

19 August 1851, *Journal* 3: 378–79

We cannot write well or truly but what we write with gusto. The body the senses must conspire with the spirit — Expression is the act of the whole man. that our speech may be vascular — The intellect is powerless to express thought without the aid of the heart & liver of every member — Often I feel that my head stands out too dry — when it should be immersed. A writer a man writing is the scribe of all nature — he is the corn & the grass & the atmosphere writing. It is always essential that we love to do what we are doing — do it with a heart.

2 September 1851, *Journal* 4: 27–28

Men have a respect for scholarship and learning greatly out of proportion to the use they commonly serve. We are amused to read how Ben Jonson engaged, that the dull masks with which the royal family and nobility were to be entertained, should be "grounded upon antiquity and solid learning." Can there be any greater reproach than an idle learning? Learn to split wood at least. The necessity of labor and conversation with many men and things, to the scholar is rarely well remembered; steady labor with the hands, which engrosses the attention also, is unquestionably the best method of removing palaver and sentimentality out of one's style, both of speaking and writing. If he has worked hard from morning till night, though he may have grieved that he could not be watching the train of his thoughts during that time, yet the few hasty lines which at evening record his day's experience will be more musical and true than his freest but idle fancy could have furnished. Surely the writer is to address a world of laborers, and such therefore must be his own discipline. He will not idly dance at his work who has wood to cut and cord before night-fall in the short days of winter; but every stroke will be husbanded, and ring soberly through the wood; and so will the strokes of that scholar's pen, which at evening record the story of the day, ring soberly, yet cheerily, on the ear of the reader, long after the echoes of his axe have died away. That scholar may be sure that he writes the tougher truth for the calluses on his palms. They give firmness to the sentence. Indeed, the mind never makes a great and successful effort without a corresponding energy of the body. We are often struck by the force and precision of style to which hard-working men, unpractised in writing, easily attain, when required to make the effort. As if plainness and vigor, and sincerity, the ornaments of style, were better learned on the farm and in the workshop than in the schools. The sentences written by such rude hands are nervous and tough, like hardened thongs, the sinews of the deer, or the roots of the pine. As for the graces of expression, a great thought is never found in a mean dress; but though it proceed from the lips of the Woloffs, the nine Muses and the three Graces will have conspired to clothe it in a fit phrase. Its education has always been liberal, and its implied wit can endow a college. The world, which the Greeks called Beauty, has been made such by being gradually divested of every ornament which was not fitted to endure. The Sibyl, "speaking with inspired mouth, smileless, inornate, and unperfumed, pierces through the centuries by the power of the god." The scholar might frequently emulate the propriety and emphasis of the farmer's call to his team, and confess that if that were written it would surpass his labored sentences. Whose are the truly *labored* sentences? From the weak and flimsy periods of the politician and literary man, we are glad to turn even to the description of work, the simple record of the month's labor in the farmer's almanac, to restore our tone and spirits. A sentence should read as if its author, had he held a plow instead of a pen, could have drawn a furrow deep and straight to the end. The scholar requires hard and serious labor to give an impetus to his thought. He will learn to grasp the pen firmly so, and wield it gracefully and effectively, as an axe or a sword.

"Sunday," *A Week on the Concord and Merrimack Rivers*, 105–7

I too would fain set down something beside facts. Facts should only be as the frame to my pictures—They should be material to the mythology which I am writing. Not facts to assist men to make money—farmers to farm profitably in any common sense. Facts to tell who I am—and where I have been—or what I have thought. As now the bell rings for evening meeting—& its volumes of sound like smoke which rises from where a cannon is fired—make the tent in which I dwell. My facts shall all be falsehoods to the common sense. I would so state facts that they shall be significant shall be myths or mythologic. Facts which the mind perceived—thoughts which the body thought with these I deal.

9 November 1851, *Journal* 4: 170

I fear chiefly lest my expression may not be *extra- vagant* enough, may not wander far enough beyond the narrow limits of my daily experience, so to be adequate to the truth of which I have been convinced. *Extra vagance*! it depends on how you are yarded. The migrating buffalo, which seeks new pastures in another latitude, is not extravagant like the cow which kicks over the pail, leaps the cow fence, and runs after her calf, in milking time. I desire to speak somewhere *without* bounds; like a man in a waking moment, to men in their waking moments; for I am convinced that I cannot exaggerate enough even to lay the foundation of a true expression. Who that has heard a strain of music feared then lest he should speak extravagantly any more forever? In view of the future or possible, we should live quite laxly and undefined in front, our outlines dim and misty on that side; as our shadows reveal an insensible perspiration toward the sun. The volatile truth of our words should continually betray the inadequacy of the residual statement. Their truth is instantly *translated*; its literal monument alone remains. The words which express our faith and piety are not definite; yet they are significant and fragrant like frankincense to superior natures.

"Conclusion," *Walden,* 324–25

One young man of my acquaintance, who has inherited some acres, told me that he thought he should live as I did, *if he had the means.* I would not have any one adopt *my* mode of living on any account; for beside that before he has fairly learned it I may have found out another for myself. I desire that there may be as many different persons in the world as possible; but I would have each one be very careful to find out and pursue *his own* way, and not his father's or his mother's or his neighbor's instead. The youth may build or plant or sail, only let him not be hindered from doing that which he tells me he would like to do. It is by a mathematical point only that we are wise, as the sailor or the fugitive slave keeps the polestar in his eye; but that is sufficient guidance for all our life. We may not arrive at our port within a calculable period, but we would preserve the true course.

"Economy," *Walden,* 71

I learned this, at least, by my experiment; that if one advances confidently in the direction of his dreams, and endeavors to live the life which he has imagined, he will meet with a success unexpected in common hours. He will put some things behind, will pass an invisible boundary; new, universal, and more liberal laws will begin to establish themselves around and within him; or the old laws be expanded, and interpreted in his favor in a more liberal sense, and he will live with the license of a higher order of beings. In proportion as he simplifies his life, the laws of the universe will appear less complex, and solitude will not be solitude, nor poverty poverty, nor weakness weakness. If you have built castles in the air, your work need not be lost; that is where they should be. Now put the foundations under them.

"Conclusion," *Walden,* 323–24

Further Reading

The Spirit of Thoreau

Further Reading

Works by Thoreau

The Correspondence of Henry David Thoreau. Edited by Walter Harding and Carl Bode. New York: New York University Press, 1958. Reprint, Westport, Conn.: Greenwood, 1974.

Early Essays and Miscellanies. Edited by Joseph J. Moldenhauer and Edwin Moser, with Alex C. Kern. Princeton: Princeton University Press, 1975.

Excursions. Boston: Houghton Mifflin, 1863.

The Journal of Henry David Thoreau. Volumes I–XIV. Edited by Bradford Torrey and Francis H. Allen. Boston: Houghton Mifflin, 1906.

Journal. Volumes 1–5. General editor, Robert Sattelmeyer. Princeton: Princeton University Press, 1981–1997.

The Natural History Essays. Edited by Robert Sattel-meyer. Salt Lake City: Peregrine Smith, 1980.

Reform Papers. Edited by Wendell Glick. Princeton: Princeton University Press, 1973.

Walden. Edited by Lyndon D. Shanley. Princeton: Princeton University Press, 1971.

A Week on the Concord and Merrimack Rivers. Edited by Carl F. Hovde, William Howarth, and Elizabeth Hall Witherell. Princeton: Princeton University Press, 1980.

NOTE: Thoreau's journal exists in two editions. The more recent and more accurate Princeton edition, though, is still in progress, complete only to March 1853. Where possible, I have used this edition, indicated by an arabic numeral for the volume number; elsewhere the Houghton Mifflin edition is used, indicated by a roman-numeral volume number.

OTHER WORKS CITED
AND SECONDARY SOURCES

Adams, Raymond. "Thoreau: Pioneer in Adult Education." *Institute Magazine* 3 (1930): 6–7.

Albee, John. *Remembrances of Emerson.* New York: R. G. Cooke, 1901.

Alcott, Amos Bronson. *Conversations with Children on the Gospels.* Boston: James Munroe and Company, 1836–37.

———. *Essays on Education.* Edited by Walter Harding. Gainesville, Fla.: Scholars' Facsimiles, 1960.

Alcott, Louisa May. *Little Men: Life at Plumfield with Jo's Boys.* Boston: Roberts Brothers, 1871.

Dennison, George. *The Lives of Children: The Story of the First Street School.* Reading, Mass.: Addison-Wesley, 1969.

Dewey, John. "John Dewey on Thoreau." *Thoreau Society Bulletin* (1950): 1.

Emerson, Edward Waldo. *Henry Thoreau as Remembered by a Young Friend.* Boston: Houghton Mifflin, 1917.

Emerson, Ralph Waldo. *Emerson in His Journals.* Edited by Joel Porte. Cambridge: Harvard University Press, 1982.

———. *Essays and Lectures.* Edited by Joel Porte. New York: Library of America, 1983.

Harding, Walter. "Henry D. Thoreau, Instructor." *Educational Forum* 24 (1964): 89–97.

Hughes, Mildred P. "Thoreau as Writer and Teacher of Writing." *English Journal* 67 (1978): 33–35.

Hurd, Harry Elmore. "Henry David Thoreau—A Pioneer in the Field of Education." *Education* 49 (1929): 372–76.

O'Connor, Dick. "Thoreau in the Town School, 1837." *Concord Saunterer,* new series 4 (1996): 150–72.

Peabody, Elizabeth. *Record of a School: Exemplifying the General Principles of Spiritual Culture.* Boston: James Munroe and Company, 1835.

Pinkston, Joan W. "Thoreau and Current Trends in the Teaching of Writing." *English Journal* 78 (1989): 50–52.

Ryan, Kevin. "Henry David Thoreau: Critic, Theorist, and Practitioner of Education." *School Review* (1969): 54–63.

Salomon, Louis B. "The Straight-Cut Ditch: Thoreau on Education." *American Quarterly* 14 (1962): 19–36.

Sanborn, F. B. *The Life of Henry David Thoreau.* Boston: Houghton Mifflin, 1917.

Willson, Lawrence. "Thoreau on Education." *History of Education Quarterly* 2 (1962): 19–29.

THE SPIRIT OF THOREAU

"How many a man has dated a new era in his life from the reading of a book," wrote Henry David Thoreau in *Walden*. Today that book, perhaps more than any other American work, continues to provoke, inspire, and change lives all over the world, and each rereading is fresh and challenging. Yet as Thoreau's countless admirers know, there is more to the man than *Walden*. An engineer, poet, teacher, naturalist, lecturer, and political activist, he truly had several lives to lead, and each one speaks forcefully to us today.

The Spirit of Thoreau introduces the thoughts of a great writer on a variety of important topics, some that we readily associate him with, some that may be surprising. Each book includes selections from his familiar published works as well as from less well known and even previously unpublished lectures, letters, and journal entries. Thoreau claimed that "to read well, that is, to read true books in a true spirit, is a noble exercise, and one that will task the reader more than any exercise which the customs of the day esteem." The volume editors and the Thoreau Society believe that you will find these new aspects of Thoreau an exciting "exercise" indeed.

This Thoreau Society series reunites Henry Thoreau with

his historic publisher. For more than a hundred years, the venerable publishing firm of Houghton Mifflin has been associated with standard editions of the works of Emerson and Thoreau and with important bibliographical and interpretive studies of the New England Transcendentalists. Until Princeton University Press began issuing new critical texts in *The Writings of Henry D. Thoreau*, beginning with *Walden* in 1971, Thoreauvians were well served by Houghton Mifflin's twenty-volume Walden or Manuscript Edition of *The Writings of Henry David Thoreau* (1906). Having also published Walter Harding's annotated edition of *Walden* (1995), Houghton Mifflin is again in the forefront of Thoreau studies.

You are invited to continue exploring Thoreau by joining our society. For well over fifty years we have presented publications, annual gatherings, and other programs to further the appreciation of Thoreau's thought and writings. And now we have embarked on a bold new venture. In partnership with the Walden Woods Project, the Thoreau Society has formed the Thoreau Institute, a research and educational center housing the world's greatest collection of materials by and about Thoreau. In ways that the author of *Walden* could not have imagined, his message is still changing lives in a brand-new era.

For membership information, write to the Thoreau Society, 44 Baker Farm, Lincoln, MA 01773-3004, or call 781-259-4750. To learn more about the Thoreau Institute, write to the same address; call 781-259-4700; or visit the Web site:

www.walden.org.

WESLEY T. MOTT
Series Editor
The Thoreau Society